SMSF PROPERTY MASTERY

Build Wealth, Save Tax, and Take Control of Your Retirement

Robbie Joseph

Copyright

Edition: 2026

ISBN: 978-1-7637686-4-2

Dedication:

I dedicate this book to my children, Emma and Samuel Joseph. Further, I dedicate this book to the power and love of our lord Jesus Christ in my life, without whom, this book would not have been possible.

Table of Contents

Introduction:

In recent years, investing in property through Self-Managed

Superannuation Funds (SMSFs) has grown in popularity as a strategic method for building long-term wealth. While the primary focus of superannuation is on securing a comfortable retirement, SMSFs offer individuals flexibility and control to manage their investments, and property is one of the most effective ways to capitalise on this opportunity.

This book is designed to offer both new and experienced investors a comprehensive guide to SMSF property investments. Whether you are considering purchasing your first property or expanding an existing portfolio, this guide will walk you through the benefits, risks, and strategies involved. From understanding tax efficiencies to choosing the right type of property, the insights provided here will help you make informed decisions to maximise your retirement savings.

By leveraging the unique benefits offered by SMSFs, such as concessional tax rates, superannuation contributions as a funding method, and property ownership within a protected environment, you can strategically position yourself for long-term financial independence. This book aims to simplify the complexities of SMSF property investments, offering practical examples, case studies, and expert guidance to help you succeed.

Whether you are an individual looking to diversify your super investments or a seasoned investor seeking advanced strategies, the lessons contained here will give you the tools and confidence needed to grow your wealth through SMSF property investments.

About the Author: A Journey of SMSF Success

My name is Robbie Joseph, and for the past 20 years, I have dedicated my career to helping individuals and businesses make the most of their Self-Managed Super Funds (SMSFs).

I have always been a passionate advocate of property investment for wealth creation purposes, given the low taxation and exemptions from paying Capital Gains Tax in the pension phase. Buying property in an SMSF comes with many benefits. I believe that if done correctly and for the right objectives, it can be one of the most beneficial strategies for purchasing property to create retirement wealth and income.

FACT *According to the ATO's latest statistics (December 2024), SMSFs now hold $168 billion in direct property, which accounts for 16.5% of all SMSF assets. Earlier industry data suggested that around 15% of SMSFs held direct property, with approximately 80% of that being commercial and 20% residential, according to the Australian Taxation Office.*

I will show you how to purchase property in an SMSF so you can enjoy some of these benefits:

- *No impact on your personal income or lifestyle.*
- *Pay 22% less tax* on income, and 0% capital gains tax.*
- *Pay off your loan in two-thirds of the time compared to a property held outside of super.*

This book is a reflection of the knowledge I have gained over nearly two decades of working with SMSFs and property investors. It is a guide to not only help you understand the mechanics of SMSF property investments but also to show you how these strategies can be customised to fit your specific financial goals. Let us get started on building your path to a secure and prosperous retirement through smart, strategic SMSF property investment.

Contributor Profile

Dinesh Nanayakkara, SSAud
Principal Auditor, D.S Audit Services

Dinesh Nanayakkara is the Principal Auditor and founder of D.S Audit Services, a leading independent audit firm specialising in *Self-Managed Superannuation Fund (SMSF)* compliance. As an SMSF Specialist Auditor (SSAud), Dinesh brings extensive expertise in statutory audits, financial reporting standards, and superannuation law.

With a strong technical background and a meticulous approach to professional integrity, Dinesh has worked with accountants, trustees, and financial professionals across Australia to ensure funds meet the rigorous obligations of the *Superannuation Industry (Supervision) Act 1993* (SIS Act) and associated regulations.

In this book, Dinesh contributes his insights in *Chapter 12: Audit Requirements for SMSF Property Investments*, providing readers with practical guidance on documentation, evidence management, and audit readiness for property-related investments within SMSFs. His expertise adds an essential compliance and assurance perspective to the strategies presented throughout this blueprint.

Why SMSFs?

Self-Managed Superannuation Funds (SMSFs) are unique in Australia's retirement system. They are the only vehicles that gives members direct ownership and control over their retirement assets. By contrast, in retail and industry super funds, members are only beneficial owners, relying on external trustees and managers to make investment decisions on their behalf.

This distinction matters because of Australia's evolving financial framework. In 2018, the government passed the *Financial Sector Legislation Amendment (Crisis Resolution Powers and Other Measures) Act*, which granted the Australian Prudential Regulation Authority (APRA) expanded "crisis resolution" powers. Critics argue that these provisions, sometimes described as "bail-in" laws, could allow regulators to intervene in banks and financial institutions during a crisis.

While official statements maintain that retail deposits and superannuation balances are not intended to be subject to bail-in, some legal experts warn that ambiguities exist. At the very least, Australians should be aware that retail and industry super funds sit within a regulatory framework where government access in times of systemic stress is possible. SMSFs, on the other hand, are trust structures with member-trustees directly holding the assets, making them an attractive option for those who want maximum transparency and control.

The Benefits of SMSFs

SMSFs deliver clear advantages for those willing to take on the extra responsibility:

- **Low Taxation:** concessional tax rates of 15% on income and capital gains.
- **Deductible Fees:** the fund itself claims administration costs, unlike retail and industry funds.
- **Choice of Investments:** from property to shares, gold, and even cryptocurrency.
- **Clear Ownership and Control:** members directly own the fund's assets, simplifying estate planning and succession.
- **Multiple Income Streams:** super contributions, rental income, dividends, and interest.

The Risks of SMSFs

But SMSFs are not without their challenges:

- **Greater Responsibility:** trustees must comply with super and tax law.
- **Time Commitment:** regular administration and record-keeping are essential for the fund to remain compliant.
- **Suitability:** not all Australians have sufficient super savings, experience, or interest to manage an SMSF effectively.

Australia's Love Affair with Property

Few things define Australian wealth like property. According to the ABS, around 66% of Australian households own their home, one of the highest property ownership rates globally. Property is deeply embedded in the national psyche, representing stability, wealth creation, and family security.

An SMSF provides a unique way to tap into this love of property. With the ability to borrow under limited recourse arrangements (super fund loans or LRBAs), members can acquire property within their super, backed by concessional super contributions to help service the loan. The benefit of this approach is that repayments are supported by super contributions and rental income, meaning little, if any, impact on household cash flow or personal budgets.

In this book, I will guide you through SMSF property strategies from setting up the right structure to financing, compliance, and long-term wealth planning. Whether you are considering your first SMSF property purchase or want to refine your fund's strategy, this book is designed to help you make informed decisions and maximise the opportunities available through Australia's most flexible superannuation structure.

CHAPTER 1: Why SMSF Property?

Investing in property through a Self-Managed Super Fund (SMSF) offers an exciting opportunity to enhance your retirement savings by diversifying into property, which offers greater control of your financial future. By combining the power of property investment with the tax efficiencies and flexibility provided by an SMSF, you can significantly grow your wealth.

This chapter outlines the seven key benefits of investing in property through an SMSF, demonstrating why it is such a compelling option for long-term investors. These advantages range from substantial tax savings to asset protection, and from leveraging super contributions to building a diversified and controlled portfolio.

By combining the super savings and compulsory super contributions of one to six family members, most Australians can purchase property within a Self-Managed Super Fund (SMSF) to build wealth and create retirement income.

Provided you are receiving or making super contributions (currently 12% of your salary or wage), those contributions, together with the rental income from the property, are concessionally taxed at only 15%. This income is often sufficient to service a loan taken out by the SMSF to purchase property.

Buying property outside super typically requires large savings for upfront costs and sufficient income to cover the shortfall between loan repayments (interest) and the property's rental income. For many families, this can mean sacrificing lifestyle or committing additional personal income, on top of maintenance costs.

In contrast, because super contributions are mandatory and paid in addition to salary or wages, these contributions, combined with rental income, mean that an SMSF property can often be cash flow positive. This reduces or eliminates the need to use personal income to fund loan repayments, which is usually required when buying property outside super.

Another key benefit comes at retirement, when an SMSF property is sold in pension phase (after age 55 to 60, depending on your preservation age):

- No capital gains tax (CGT) is payable on the sale of the property.
- Rental income is tax-free (0%) while in the pension phase.
- If the property remains in the accumulation phase, the income continues to be concessionally taxed at 15%, much lower than personal tax rates outside super.

3 REASONS TO USE AN SMSF TO BUY YOUR FIRST OR SECOND PROPERTY

1 THREE STREAMS OF INCOME – ALL TAXED AT JUST 15%

- Super contributions
- Rental income
- Interest or dividends

compared with 37% outside super personally

2 NO IMPACT ON YOUR LIFESTYLE

Unlike most investment property that requires supplementation from personal income

3 ASSET PROTECTION AND FAMILY SUCCESSION

Property held in an SMSF is protected and can be passed down to heirs

Tax Efficiency: Reducing Your Tax Burden

One of the most powerful reasons to invest in property through an SMSF is the concessional tax treatment these funds enjoy. Unlike personal property investments, where rental income and capital gains are taxed at your marginal rate (often around 37%), SMSFs benefit from a flat tax rate of 15% on rental income and capital gains during the accumulation phase, and 0% once the fund enters the pension phase. Additionally, capital gains tax (CGT) is reduced to 10% for properties held longer than twelve months or completely eliminated during the pension phase. This makes property investments within an SMSF significantly more tax-efficient than traditional personal property investments.

Tax Category	Individual Investor (2025 MTR)	SMSF (Accumulation Phase)	SMSF (Pension Phase)
Rental Income	~37% effective	15%	0%
Capital Gains (>12 months)	Up to 23.5% effective (after discount)	10% (⅓ discount rule)	0%

The table clearly illustrates the significant tax benefits of using an SMSF to invest in property, particularly in the pension phase when both rental income and capital gains are entirely tax-free.

Using Super Contributions for Loan Repayments

A unique feature of SMSF property investment is the ability to use superannuation contributions to service property loans. With the current employer *Super Guarantee* contribution rate at 12%, these contributions can be directed into the SMSF to help cover loan repayments.

Unlike personal property loans, where repayments must come from post-tax income, SMSF loan repayments can be made using concessional super contributions along with the rental property income, which is taxed at 15% compared with income received personally, where the average marginal tax rate is 37%*. This creates a highly tax-efficient method for repaying debt and building equity in the property over time.

Case Example: Using Super Contributions for Loan Repayments

The *Super Guarantee* (SG) is 12% in 2025. For a couple earning $140,000 combined, that means $16,800 contributed annually into super before tax. Inside an SMSF, these contributions can be used to service property loans.

Loan Repayment Source	Personal Property Investment	SMSF Property Investment
Income used	After-tax salary/wages	Employer + personal concessional contributions
Tax on income	Marginal rates (up to 47 %)	Flat 15% inside SMSF
Super Guarantee contributions	Not available	$16,100 p.a. (before tax)

Observation: This structural difference allows SMSF trustees to pay down loans faster, without dipping into personal after-tax savings.

Enhanced Asset Protection: Securing Your Investments

Another significant advantage of SMSF property investments is the enhanced level of asset protection they offer, where a trustee company acts as trustee for the SMSF. Assets within an SMSF are protected from creditors and cannot be seized in the event of bankruptcy. This protection is crucial for individuals in high-risk professions, such as business owners or medical professionals, who want to safeguard their investments.

In addition, when borrowing to invest in property, SMSFs use *Limited Recourse Borrowing Arrangements* (LRBAs), which limit the lender's recourse to only the property being purchased, thereby protecting the SMSF's other assets.

Asset Type	Protection in Personal Name	Protection in SMSF
Property	Subject to creditor claims	Protected under SMSF rules
Other Assets (e.g., shares)	Subject to bankruptcy proceedings	Safeguarded within the SMSF

.

This table highlights how SMSF property investments are protected from personal creditors and other financial risks, providing a secure environment for long-term investment.

Diversification into Tangible and Alternative Assets

SMSFs allow trustees to diversify beyond traditional investments like shares and bonds into tangible and alternative assets such as property, Bitcoin, gold, and collectables. This flexibility helps balance risk and return while providing greater control and alignment with each member's investment philosophy.

Investing in tangible assets like real estate and gold can stabilise long-term returns, while assets such as Bitcoin add growth potential and diversification against inflation or currency debasement. Meanwhile, carefully selected collectables (art, jewellery, vintage cars, etc.) can offer unique appreciation opportunities provided they meet strict *SIS Act* compliance rules.

Asset Class	Volatility	Control in SMSF	Key Characteristics
Shares / Equities	High	Limited (via managed funds or brokers)	Liquidity and growth potential, but market-sensitive
Property	Medium	Full control	Tangible asset with rental income and stable growth
Bitcoin / Crypto-currencies	Very High	Full control via exchange or cold wallet	High growth, hedge against fiat inflation, and must maintain compliance
Gold / Precious Metals	Low–Medium	Full control (stored via secure vault or ETF)	Hedge against inflation and market volatility
Cash / Bonds	Low	Full control over allocation	Safe, low-return assets for liquidity and stability
Collectables (art, wine, diamonds, coins)	Medium–High	Full control (with ATO compliance)	Must meet storage and insurance rules; no personal use

Key Insight

By combining growth assets like Bitcoin and property with stability assets like gold, cash, or bonds, an SMSF can achieve a balanced portfolio that supports both long-term growth and capital preservation. Diversification across these asset types helps reduce volatility, spread risk, and improve overall fund performance, all while giving trustees direct control over how their retirement wealth is managed.

Growth and Reduced Risk

SMSFs can enhance the growth potential of property investments by using *Limited Recourse Borrowing Arrangements* (LRBAs). This form of borrowing limits the lender's recourse to the property itself, protecting other fund assets and ensuring that members' personal wealth outside super is not at risk.

Leverage allows SMSFs to purchase larger or higher-quality assets than would otherwise be possible, which can amplify investment growth. Over the long term, property values in Australia have historically trended upwards, meaning the compounding effect of leveraged growth can be substantial.

Importantly, superannuation assets benefit from a longer investment horizon. Because contributions are mandatory and continue to flow into the fund regardless of market conditions, and as the funds are only accessible at age 55 to 60. For these reasons, SMSFs are often better positioned to ride out property market cycles.

Even if there is a temporary downturn, the combination of contributions and rental income provides servicing capacity without impacting members' personal income or lifestyle. This reduces the risk of being forced to sell an asset prematurely in a market downturn to meet loan repayments, which is a common risk with property held outside super.

In essence, SMSF leverage offers a unique balance: the potential for higher growth through borrowing, coupled with the security of limited recourse, steady super contributions, and the tax concessions available only in the super environment.

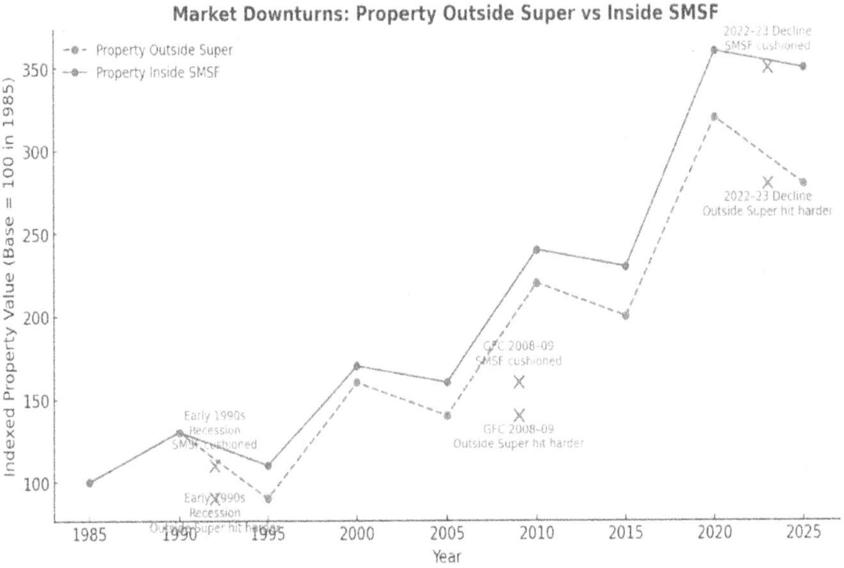

Comparison of owning Property personally versus via an SMSF

Comparison of owning Property personaily versus via an SMSF

	Self-owned	**SMSF**	**Savings**
Starting balance in SMSF	–	$150.000	$0
Property Purchase price	$420.000	$420.000	$420.000
Property value (15yrs later)	$820.000	$820.000	$0
Deposit	$42.000	$126.000	$126.000
Gross Capital Gain	210.000 x 45%		280.000 x 15%
Tax on sale proceeds (CGT)	$94.500	$42.000⁺	$52.500
Stamp Duty⁺ (NSW)	13.663.40	13.663.40	13.663.42
Net Capital Gain	449.566	$657.027	$207.462
Loan interest saving (Yrs.)	30	20	10 years
Loan interest saved	$586.445	$293.998	$292.447
Rental Returns	–	$91.520	**$436.467**
Total Savings with Strategy			**$436.467**

*Assumption NSW apartment purchased in 2025 in Carrarnarar

When an SMSF borrows, it uses a Limited Recourse Borrowing Arrangement (LRBA). This magnifies growth potential by allowing the fund to acquire larger assets.

Direct Control and Flexibility: Tailoring Your Strategy

An SMSF offers greater control and flexibility than traditional superannuation funds, where investment decisions are made by fund managers. With an SMSF, you can directly control which properties to buy, how they are financed, and when to sell, allowing you to tailor your investment strategy to meet your specific financial goals.

Investment Decision	Traditional Super Fund	SMSF
Property Selection	No control	Full control
Loan Structure	No control	Full control over financing
Exit Strategy	Managed by fund	Self-managed

The table clearly shows the degree of control and flexibility SMSF investors have, particularly when it comes to property investment decisions.

No Personal Financial Strain

Investing in property through an SMSF allows you to keep the investment separate from your personal income and financial situation. The property is held by the SMSF, and the loan repayments can be covered by the SMSF's income, such as rental income and superannuation contributions. This approach prevents the investment from placing a strain on your personal cash flow.

Comparison of Repayment Sources – Personal vs SMSF Property Investment

Investment Type	Repayment Sources	Typical Income Streams	Impact on Personal Cash Flow
Personal Property Investment	Personal income + rental income	- Personal income (salary/wag-es) - Rental income from property	High – must cover loan repayments from post-tax personal income if rental income income is insufficient
SMSF Property Investment	SMSF income (contribu-tions, rental income, interest, and dividend earnings)	- Super contributions (employer & personal concessional) - Rental income from SMSF property - Investment earnings (interest/ dividends from other SMSF assets)	Low – repayments funded funded within SMSF, minimal to no direct impact on personal cash flow

This table highlights how SMSF property investments reduce the financial strain on personal finances, as the investment is entirely funded by the SMSF.

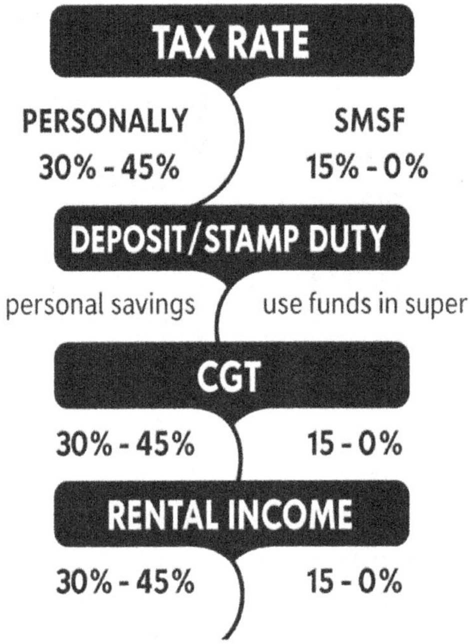

Case Study: A Couple aged 55, combined $140,000 income.

Assumptions

- Husband earns $90,000, wife $50,000.
- Home already owned, no mortgage.
- $150,000 super saved between them.

- Buying a property worth $420,000 in Carramar, NSW
- Property rental income $20,800
- SG contributions at 12%.

Case Study:

This updated scenario compares the same $420,000 and rental income of $20,800 property outside and inside the super.

Funding Component	Outside Super	Inside SMSF
SMSF Balance $42,000 (10%)	Deposit $150,000	$126,000 (30%)
Loan $360,000	Interest Cost $25,762 (5.95%) *	$29,400 (7.95%)
Employer Contributions	N/A	$14,280 (after tax)
Net Rent (after tax)	$13,104	$17,680
Net Servicing Result	Deficit -$12,658	Surplus +$2,560
Stamp Duty (NSW)	$13,663.40	$13,663.40

Example 1: Rental Returns

Item	Individual (MTR 37%)	SMSF (15% tax)
Gross rental return	$20,800	$20,800
Tax payable	$7,696*	$3,120
Net rental return	**$13,104**	**$17,680**
Tax saved over 20 years		$91,520

**Assuming income does not go up*

Loan Repayment Illustration

- Loan Amount: $294,000
- Interest Rate: 7.95% P&I
- Net Rental Income: $20,000 (before tax)
- Employer Contributions: $16,100 p.a. (before tax)
- Net Super Contributions (after 15% tax): $13,685

SMSF	Net Income	Notes
Rental Income	$17,680	Net after 15% SMSF tax on $20,800
Net Super Contributions	$14,280	12% of $140k = $16,800, less 15% tax
Total Available	$31,960	Correct sum
Annual Loan Repayments	$29,400	Actual P&I at 7.95% over 20 years
Surplus	$2,560	Corrected calculation
Loan Payoff Time	~20 years	20 years vs 30 years. SMSF loan term vs typical property loan outside super
Result: Loan fully repaid in ~20 years vs ~30 years outside super.		

Costs of Setting Up an SMSF for Property (2025)

Setup Item	Cost
SMSF Setup	$990
SMSF Annual Tax/Audit	$1190
Property Trust (bare trust)	$1,550–$2,200
Lender Fees	$2,500–$3,500
Conveyancing	$1,200–$2,500

Note: While setup costs are higher than personal purchase, most are deductible to the SMSF, and long-term savings outweigh them significantly.

Funding Options

Option 1 – SMSF Loan (LRBA)

- **Advantages:** No LMI, recourse limited to property.
- **Disadvantages:** Higher rates, higher setup, and liquidity test.

Option 2 – Related Party Loan

- **Advantages:** Lower costs, interest deductible at a higher personal tax rate.
- **Disadvantages:** Requires personal security, risk of double gearing.

Summary

- **Rental Tax Savings:** $91,520 over 20 years
- **Loan Repayment:** 20 years inside super vs 30 outside.
- **CGT Savings:** 94,500*when property sold in pension phase.

- **Cash Flow:** Surplus inside SMSF, annual deficit outside.

Conclusion: Investing in property through an SMSF provides tax efficiency, cash flow strength, asset protection, and long-term growth.

Footnotes:

***Property value assumption:** *Based on conservative 15-year doubling projection (4.73% p.a.), well below Sydney's historical average of 7-7.5% p.a. Sources: Prop Track Market Insights 2023, CoreLogic Home Value Index 2025, Reserve Bank of Australia Bulletin 2015.* ***CGT in pension phase:** *0% (no capital gains tax)*

Key SMSF Advantages:

1. LIFESTYLE PRESERVATION

- **Outside Super:** Must save $42,000 from after-tax personal income, reducing lifestyle and spending capacity.
- **SMSF:** Uses existing super balance — **no impact on lifestyle or personal cash flow.**

2. TAX EFFICIENCY

- **Rental income:** 15% vs 37% tax = **$68,640 saved over 15 years**
- **Capital gains:** 15% vs 45% tax = **$52,500 saved**
- **In pension phase:** 0% tax on rent and capital gains!

3. WEALTH ACCELERATION

- **$207,462 more net equity** after 15 years
- Loan paid off **10 years earlier** (20 vs 30 years)
- **$154,962 less debt** at the 15-year mark

4. STRATEGIC ADVANTAGES

- Leverage **accumulated super** without lifestyle sacrifice
- Most Australians already have super — no need to save separately.
- Super **contributions are concessionally taxed** (tax-deductible)
- Transition to **pension phase for 0% tax** on everything
- Asset protection within a superannuation structure

The Bottom Line:

Buying property through an SMSF allows you to:

- Use money you've **already saved** (accumulated super)
- Pay **significantly less tax** (15% vs 37-45%)
- Build **$207,462 more wealth** over 15 years.
- Achieve all this **without impacting your lifestyle or personal spending.**

This is why SMSFs are one of the most powerful wealth-building strategies available to Australians.

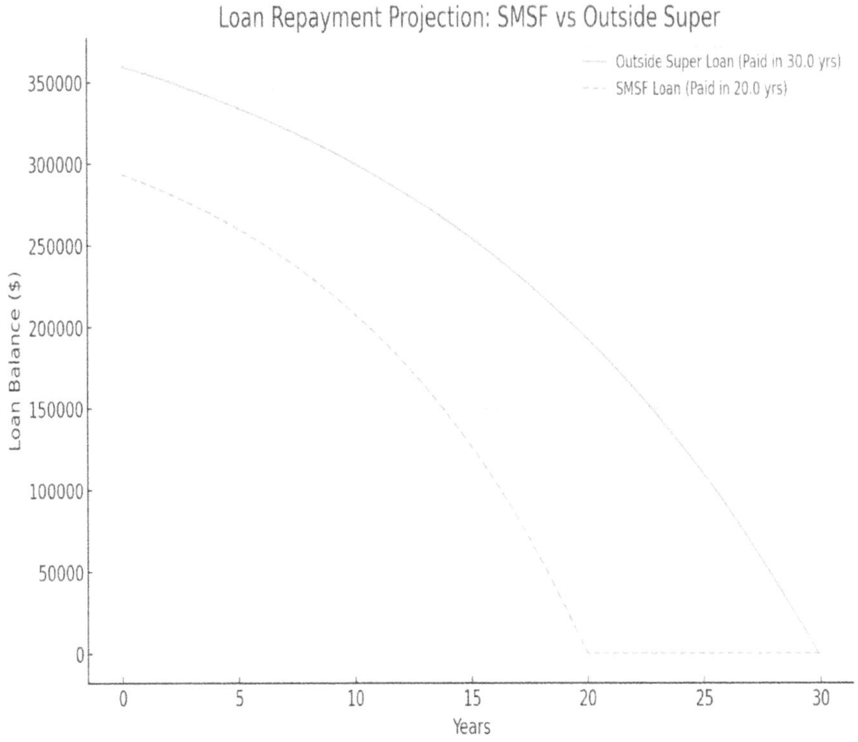

This table illustrates the significant difference in returns when leveraging property investments through an SMSF compared to investing without leverage.

SMSF Property Strategy Details:

How it works

Investing in property through a Self-Managed Super Fund (SMSF) can feel complex, but it is essentially about putting the right pieces in place in the right order. Think of it like assembling a model house: your SMSF provides the foundation (deposit), a special trust (bare trust) holds the house, a lender helps with a loan, and the rent collected helps pay it off. In this section, I will walk through each step in plain English, from setting up your SMSF and funding it to creating the *bare trust*, arranging the loan, signing contracts correctly, settling the purchase, and managing the property thereafter. Along the way, I will highlight key compliance tips (like avoiding double stamp duty) and show why, when done right, buying property in an SMSF can be so rewarding.

Figure: Example structure of an SMSF property purchase.

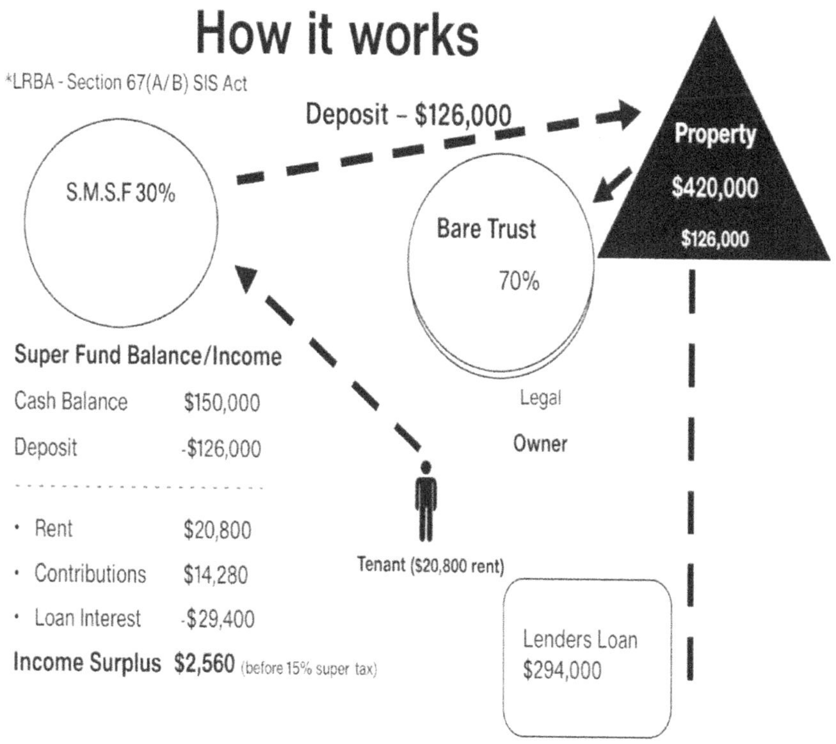

1. Setting Up Your SMSF (Laying the Foundations)

First, you need a properly established SMSF to undertake a property purchase. If you do not already have one, this means creating the SMSF, identifying member trustees for the fund, getting an SMSF trust deed in place, and then registering with the ATO for the fund's ABN/TFN, and rollovers from any existing super funds.

As part of this setup, you will also draft an investment strategy for your SMSF, ensuring it permits property investment and borrowing under an LRBA (Limited Recourse Borrowing Arrangement). Most SMSFs have a corporate trustee (a company set up to act as trustee) because it offers administrative ease, is preferred by lenders, and comes with greater security. In short, get all the groundwork done so your SMSF is legally ready and allowed to buy property.

Compliance reminder: SMSFs exist solely to provide retirement benefits, so any property you buy must be for investment purposes only. You and your relatives cannot live in it or rent it for personal use. For example, buying a holiday house through your SMSF that you or your kids plan to stay in is strictly off-limits. The property also generally cannot be bought from a related party (with a limited exception for certain business real estate). These rules are part of the "sole purpose test," essentially making sure your SMSF's property is purely a retirement nest egg asset, not a lifestyle perk.

2. Funding the SMSF (Building Your Deposit)

Once your SMSF is up and running, it needs enough money in it to cover a property deposit and related costs. Remember, all funding for the purchase must come from within the SMSF, but you can make additional contributions from savings (up to the contribution cap levels) and the sale of other assets after tax to top up your SMSF to meet any requirements.

Typically, SMSF loans require a larger deposit than ordinary home loans. As a rule of thumb, many banks ask for about 30% of the property value as a deposit (meaning they will finance roughly 70%). You will also need extra in the SMSF to pay for stamp duty, legal fees, and other purchase costs, plus a buffer for ongoing expenses.

Funding your SMSF can come from rolling over existing super balances (if you have, say, $200k in a retail or industry fund, you might transfer that into the SMSF). You and any other members can also make contributions (within the annual contribution limits) to boost the balance. For example, if two members each salary-sacrifice some of their income into super, those contributions can help build the war chest for the property.

Planning this funding is crucial; often, SMSF investors consult a financial planner or SMSF specialist mortgage broker at this stage to determine how much they can afford to spend on a property and how much to borrow. The goal is to ensure the SMSF will have enough cash flow to comfortably support the loan repayments before committing to a purchase.

Real-world example: Suppose your SMSF has $150,000 available. You target a property worth $420,000. Your SMSF might use about $126,000 as a 30% deposit and then borrow approximately $294,000 (70%) from a lender to make up the rest. You would set aside additional funds for stamp duty and closing costs (say $20,000, varying by state/price). After the purchase, you would still want a cash buffer in the fund for safety. Never empty the SMSF entirely for the deposit, since you'll need ongoing liquidity for loan payments, fees, and any unexpected expenses.

3. Establishing the Bare Trust (Your Property's Custodian)

With your SMSF ready and cashed up for a deposit, the next step is to set up a Bare Trust (also known as a custodian or holding trust). This is a special trust that will hold the property on behalf of your SMSF while there is a loan against the property. The bare trust exists solely for this purpose; it does nothing else (hence "bare"). Think of it as a nominee or custodian: like a trusted friend holding the property title for you until your mortgage is paid off.

Setting up a bare trust involves drafting a bare trust deed and usually establishing a corporate trustee for this trust (often a newly created company whose only job is to act as trustee of the bare trust). The SMSF trustee cannot be the trustee of the bare trust – they must be separate entities. In fact, many lenders insist that both the SMSF trustee and the bare trustee are companies for ease of dealing and to avoid any overlap.

Don't worry, your SMSF still beneficially owns the property – the bare trust is purely a legal technicality to satisfy super law and lender requirements. Under an LRBA arrangement, the bare trustee will hold the property title and the mortgage in its name on behalf of the SMSF. This structure provides an extra layer of protection: if the loan ever went bad, the bank's "recourse" is limited to the property in the bare trust, and creditors cannot seize other assets of your SMSF. In a way, the bare trust acts like a safety container around the property.

It is important to have a lawyer or SMSF service provider set up the bare trust correctly and (in many states) arrange for the trust deed to be stamped or lodged with the state revenue office. The timing of signing and stamping the bare trust deed can be critical to avoid stamp duty issues, noting that requirements differ by state (in some states, the deed is signed before the property contract, in others shortly after, etc.), so getting legal guidance here is wise.

In summary, the bare trust is your SMSF property's legal owner on paper, but it has no independent will of its own; it acts purely at the SMSF's direction. It is like a holding bay for the property until the loan is paid off. Once the loan is fully repaid down the track, the property title can be transferred from the bare trust to the SMSF properly, usually with minimal or no stamp duty because the beneficial ownership has not changed.

4. Arranging the Limited Recourse Loan (LRBA)

Now, to finance the rest of the purchase: your SMSF will borrow the remaining funds through a Limited Recourse Borrowing Arrangement (LRBA). This is basically a fancy term for a loan to your SMSF that has special conditions. "Limited recourse" means the lender's claims are limited to the asset itself (the property held in the bare trust). If the SMSF defaults, the bank can seize only that property as collateral, not any other assets in your SMSF. This is crucial (and actually mandated by law) to protect the rest of your retirement savings from a worst-case scenario. It also explains why the structure is the way it is: the bank gets comfort by having the property in a separate trust they can access, and your SMSF gets comfort (and a legal requirement) that the rest of its assets are off-limits to the bank.

To set up the LRBA loan, you will typically work with a bank or specialised lender that offers SMSF loans. (Not all lenders do, and terms can be a bit stricter than regular home loans.) It's often wise to engage a mortgage broker experienced in SMSF lending to shop around for a good rate and terms. The lender will assess your SMSF's situation much like a normal loan application, looking at the fund's income (contributions + rental income expected), existing assets, the property's expected rent, etc. They may also require personal guarantees from the SMSF members/trustees, since the loan is limited recourse to the property (many banks want an extra layer of assurance, effectively having you as a member promise to be responsible if the fund cannot pay). This does not void the limited recourse, but it is an additional security for them.

During this stage, you will seek pre-approval for the loan if possible, so you know how much the SMSF can borrow before you go property shopping. Let us say the lender approves a loan for up to $300,000 for that $420,000 property example, which aligns with your SMSF having to put in roughly $120k–$130k plus costs. The interest rates on SMSF loans are usually a bit higher than owner-occupier home loans and often a bit higher than normal investment loans as well, given the limited recourse nature. Also, the loan might be interest-only for a period (some SMSF loans are interest-only for 5 or even 15 years, to keep payments lower and let your super contributions help chip away later, or plan to pay a lump sum before retirement). Make sure to factor in all these conditions.

One more thing: some lenders will have specific requirements, like insisting the SMSF trustee is a company, and the bare trust trustee is a different company (which, as mentioned, is often the case). They might also want to review the bare trust deed to ensure it meets their criteria and the SIS laws (especially that it explicitly states the limited recourse condition). This is normal; it is just the bank doing due diligence to be certain everything is compliant.

By the end of this step, you should have your loan approved (or at least formally pre-approved), ready to go when you find the property and sign a contract. Getting finance sorted is critical; with SMSFs it's prudent to have that lined up early, because you don't want to commit the SMSF to a purchase contract and then find out the loan falls through. Remember, as the SMSF trustee, you are personally responsible for the fund's obligations. A failed settlement could be a nightmare (loss of deposit, legal trouble, etc.), so treat loan arrangements with due care and get solid approval before proceeding to buy.

5. Signing the Contract (Properly!)

With your deposit ready and loan approved, your SMSF can now go ahead and purchase the property. This step is where attention to detail is absolutely critical to avoid costly mistakes. The property contract of sale must be signed in the name of the bare trust's trustee (the custodian trustee), not in the name of the SMSF or its trustees personally.

In practical terms, if your bare trust's corporate trustee is called *ABC Pty Ltd as trustee for XYZ Bare Trust*, that is the purchaser's name that should appear on the contract. This might feel odd since it's your SMSF's money, but it's required because the legal owner will be the bare trustee.

In fact, Land Titles Offices often don't record trusts themselves on title, only the trustee, which is why the bare trustee signs the contract as the legal purchaser.

Why is this so important? If you get it wrong, for example, if you or your SMSF company accidentally sign as the buyer instead of the bare trustee, you could trigger a need to transfer the property later into the correct structure, and that can mean paying stamp duty twice (once on the initial purchase and again on the transfer). Double stamp duty is a very expensive mistake, essentially a penalty for not structuring it right from the start. It's a common trap for the unwary and has even caught out professionals who aren't familiar with SMSF rules.

> **Bottom line:** make sure the contract is in the bare trustee's name at the outset and that the bare trust deed is executed around the same time as required to satisfy state laws. When done properly, the eventual transfer of title to the SMSF (after the loan is repaid) won't incur additional duty because the beneficial owner (the SMSF) was the same all along.

Given the high stakes at contract time, it is highly recommended to use a conveyancer or solicitor experienced in SMSF property purchases. They will ensure the contract is drafted correctly (with appropriate trustee wording), handle any special conditions needed for the LRBA, and lodge the bare trust deed for duty assessment if required in your state. An SMSF-savvy conveyancer will know the timing requirements between signing the bare trust deed and signing the contract to keep everything compliant and avoid that dreaded double duty.

Engaging a professional here is a small price to pay for peace of mind. Consider it like hiring a specialist surgeon for a delicate operation. The rules are nuanced, and a misstep can be costly not just in money but in legal compliance. Remember, if the loan documents and contract aren't set up correctly, the arrangement can be very hard to unwind; you might even be forced to sell the property to fix the error, which could mean major losses for your super. So, take this step seriously and lean on expert guidance.

At contract signing, your SMSF will usually need to pay the standard deposit (often 10% of the purchase price), which must come from the SMSF's bank account. Ensure those funds are readily available. After the contract is signed by all parties, you'll be locked in for settlement by the agreed date (unless subject to finance or other conditions). However, many SMSF purchases aim for finance pre-approval ahead of time to sign unconditional contracts, especially at auction. If you did make the contract "subject to finance approval," make sure to formally get that approval from the lender within the timeframe, so the contract becomes unconditional.

6. Settlement Day: Sealing the Deal

Settlement is the day the property officially changes hands. In an SMSF purchase with a loan, this is when the lender provides the loan funds and the SMSF provides the rest of the money (the balance of purchase price, stamp duty, and adjustments for rates etc.) to the seller, and in return, the property title is transferred to the bare trust's trustee (with a mortgage registered on the title in favour of the lender). It's the grand finale of the purchase process.

In preparation for settlement, your conveyancer/solicitor will coordinate with the lender. The bank will have sent loan offer documents to the SMSF trustees to sign, and typically also a mortgage for the bare trust trustee to sign (since the property is technically in the trustee's name). You might find it curious that two entities are signing: for example, *ABC Pty Ltd (*as SMSF trustee) signs the loan agreement as the borrower, and *XYZ Pty Ltd* (as bare trustee) signs the mortgage. This is normal in an LRBA: the SMSF is the borrower (it must be, since the SMSF is repaying the loan from its funds), and the bare trust gives security over the property.

On settlement day, the SMSF will draw from its bank account the remaining funds needed. Continuing our example: purchase price $420,000, 10% deposit $42,000 was paid at contract, so about $378,000 plus stamp duty/fees is due at settlement. The lender provides $294,000, and your SMSF provides the rest ($84,000 + costs). The money often flows through your solicitor or a settlement agent to the vendor.

The title will be registered to "*XYZ Pty Ltd as trustee for XYZ Bare Trust*" (or sometimes just *XYZ Pty Ltd* with an internal record of the trust beneficial owner, depending on the state), and a mortgage to the lender will be recorded. The bare trust deed will usually be noted by your lawyer for compliance, and if required, it gets stamped (e.g., in VIC a nominal duty or fee is paid on the trust deed within a certain time).

Congratulations, your SMSF now owns (indirectly, through the bare trust) an investment property. This means your SMSF's balance sheet now has a property asset (with a mortgage against it on the liability side). The hard part, the purchase, is done, but your journey as an SMSF property owner is just beginning. Now comes the ongoing management and making sure this investment works for your retirement.

7. After the Purchase: Rental Income, Loan Repayments, and Ongoing Management

Once the property is settled, your SMSF starts receiving income from it and has to manage expenses just like any landlord, all within the super fund environment. Typically, you'll appoint a property manager or manage the property yourself (via the SMSF) to find tenants, collect rent, handle maintenance, etc. All rental income must be paid into the SMSF's bank account, since the SMSF is the beneficial owner. Often, the bare trust's role is passive at this stage – it may actually be the entity listed on the lease as the landlord (since it's on the title), but the bare trustee will usually direct all rent to the SMSF. It's a good idea to have a clause or understanding in the bare trust arrangement that the SMSF is entitled to all income from the property and will cover all expenses; this is inherent, but your accountant will make sure the flow of funds reflects that beneficial ownership.

The SMSF will use the rental income, along with any other available cash (for example, contributions or other investment earnings in the fund), to pay the mortgage repayments and property costs. Loan repayments are made from the SMSF bank account – typically, you'd set up a direct debit with the lender. Keep in mind that SMSF loans often do not allow offset accounts, so any surplus cash in the SMSF can't reduce interest directly; instead, some people make additional loan repayments or hold extra cash in other investments to ensure liquidity.

You must always ensure the SMSF has enough liquidity to meet the loan and other obligations (the ATO and auditors pay attention to this). It's wise to keep a buffer of cash or liquid assets in case the property is vacant or unexpected bills come up, so you're not forced to sell assets or default.

Let us look at the cash flow in our example to see how it works: Say the property rents for $20,800 per year (which is $400 per week, roughly a 5% rental yield on $420,000). Meanwhile, the interest on the $294,000 loan at, for instance, 6.7% interest-only comes to about $19,600 per year. If rent is your only source of cash, you'd have almost no leftover after paying interest (and you'd still have outgoings like council rates, insurance, maybe property management fees!).

This is why most SMSFs rely on additional contributions or other income to support the property in our example; for example, they showed about $14,625 per year of contributions coming into the fund. With $20,800 rent + $14,600 contributions, that's $35,400 inflow. After paying $19,600 interest and, say, a few thousand in property expenses, the SMSF might have around $15,000 surplus cash flow from the property investment annually. That surplus stays in the SMSF (increasing your retirement savings), and note that it would generally be subject to only 15% tax in the SMSF if your fund is in the accumulation phase. Fifteen percent tax on $15,000 is $2,250, leaving a net ~$12,750 after-tax benefit going back into growing your super. If your SMSF is in pension phase (more on that shortly), the tax could even be zero on this income.

Of course, these numbers are just an illustration; every property's cash flow will differ. The key point is that all income and expenses from the property go through the SMSF. Your SMSF will also handle property expenses like maintenance, council rates, strata levies (if any), insurance, and property management fees. Make sure to pay all these from the SMSF's bank account (and only that account). You should never pay an SMSF property expense personally, or if you do in a pinch, have the SMSF reimburse you promptly, to avoid any issues with the sole purpose test or personal benefit rules. It is smart to keep good records of every transaction; your SMSF auditor will thank you.

If the property is positively geared (rent > expenses), the SMSF will have to pay 15% tax on the net income profit each year (until in pension phase, where it can become tax-free). If the property is negatively geared (expenses including interest > rent), then the SMSF will actually have a loss. That loss can typically offset other taxable income of the SMSF (for example, investment income from shares in the fund, or contributions tax the fund has to pay), but note that you cannot offset an SMSF's losses against your personal income outside the fund. This is different from personally held investment properties – in an SMSF, the tax benefits of negative gearing are contained within the fund. It's an important consideration in your strategy and cash flow planning.

Throughout the life of the loan, your SMSF must also meet its other obligations: annual financial statements, audits, and tax returns. The property will be valued periodically (at least every few years or when a significant event happens) to report market value to the fund members and the regulator. Ensure you comply with any LRBA requirements; for example, you cannot refinance the loan to add more borrowings for renovations that change the property (under super law, you can't improve the asset beyond its original state while under an LRBA, only repair or maintain it). Once the loan is paid down sufficiently, some SMSF investors even consider paying it off entirely using accumulated surplus or additional contributions, to then collapse the bare trust. Others might keep it going and perhaps even buy another property if their fund strategy allows.

8. Staying Compliant and Avoiding Pitfalls

SMSF property arrangements come with a lot of compliance responsibilities, so it's worth reiterating a few critical points to keep your fund out of trouble:

Bare Trust and Contract Alignment: As discussed, always have the bare trust set up and have its trustee sign any purchase contracts. The paperwork timing (trust deed vs contract) should follow state rules to avoid potential double stamp duty. If in doubt, pause and get legal guidance before signing anything. A mistaken name on the contract can be very painful to correct later.

Use Experienced Professionals: Engage an SMSF-experienced conveyancer/solicitor for property purchases. They will guide the transaction and make sure all documents (contract, trust deed, loan agreements) line up with the super law. Similarly, use a mortgage broker or banker who knows SMSFs they can navigate lender quirks and get your loan across the line more smoothly. And of course, have an SMSF-savvy accountant or advisor in the loop. This team effort will cost some fees, but it significantly lowers the risk of compliance errors. Remember, a bungled LRBA setup can be nearly impossible to unwind without selling the property at a loss, so prevention is better than cure.

Mind the SMSF Rules Post-Purchase: Continue to uphold super rules after purchase. Don't inadvertently breach rules like using the property personally (no holidays in your SMSF's rental property!), or lending money to relatives from rent, etc. Keep everything at arm's length and documented. Pay the loan on time – a default not only risks the property but could also lead to regulatory scrutiny if the fund can't meet its obligations. Also, ensure you're documenting decisions (e.g., minute a meeting of trustees approving the LRBA and property purchase) – auditors will look for that.

Plan for Liquidity: Have a strategy for funding the loan if things change. For example, if a member retires and starts drawing a pension, that will require a cash outflow from the fund – plan how the fund will manage that while still paying the mortgage (you might segregate assets or maintain a cash reserve). Also consider insurance (life/TPD) for members – if a member passed away or became disabled, the fund might need to pay out benefits, which could force a property sale if not insured. Good SMSF planning integrates these "what ifs", so the property investment remains sustainable long-term.

Conclusion

Investing in property through an SMSF offers a wealth of benefits, from tax savings, faster loan repayment, and asset protection to leveraging a retirement income stream asset and greater control over your investments. By taking advantage of these benefits, SMSF trustees can build a diversified and profitable property portfolio, positioning themselves for long-term financial independence and a secure retirement.

CHAPTER 2: Getting Started Choosing the Right Property for SMSF

When investing in property through a Self-Managed Super Fund (SMSF), selecting the right property is vital to achieving long-term financial goals. While SMSFs offer the flexibility to invest in various property types, the choice of property must align with your risk tolerance, cash flow requirements, and retirement strategy. In this chapter, I, explore the types of properties you can buy through an SMSF and offer practical guidance on selecting the right property to maximise returns while minimising risks.

Types of Properties You Can Buy with an SMSF

SMSFs can invest in a wide range of properties, provided they comply with superannuation regulations, particularly the *Sole Purpose Test* (*SIS Act* Section 62), which ensures that any investment is made solely for the purpose of providing retirement benefits to members.

Below are the main types of properties you can invest in through your SMSF:

Property Type	Description	Key Conditions / Restrictions	Opportunities & Advantages
Residential Property	Stable rental income and potential for long-term capital growth.	- Must be investment only. - No occupancy by fund members or related parties (SIS Act s62).	✔ Consistent rental yields. ✔ Easier to finance within an SMSF.
Commercial Property	Offices, warehouses, retail spaces.	- Can lease to member-owned businesses at market rates (SIS Act s66).	✔ Higher rental yields than residential. ✔ Suitable for related-party business use.
Rural & Agricultural	Farms and agricultural land.	- Leasing to related parties is allowed under conditions.	✔ Niche opportunities for those in agriculture. ✔ Potential for long-term land appreciation.
International Property	Overseas real estate.	- Must comply with Australian SMSF rules and foreign laws.	✔ Geographic diversification. ✔ Potential for foreign market growth.
Property Development	SMSF-funded development projects.	- No borrowed funds for improvements beyond original state (SIS Act s67A & s67B). - Development must use SMSF cash reserves.	✔ Adds value to existing SMSF assets. ✔ Flexibility to improve using fund cash.

SMSF Property Decision Path	
Will a member or related party use/occupy the property (even temporarily)?	→ **If yes:** Residential = no (you risk breaching the sole purpose test in SIS Act s62, because it can create a current-day benefit). → **If no:** proceed.
Are you buying the property from a related party?	→ **If yes:** Generally prohibited unless it's an exception asset (commonly "business real property"). This is the area governed by SIS Act s66 (acquisitions from related parties). → **If no:** proceed.
Do you want your business (a related party) to lease the premises?	→ **If yes:** Commercial / Business real property is often the fit – but the lease must be properly documented and on arm's length terms (SIS Act s109). → **If no:** proceed.
Is it rural/agricultural land used in a genuine business (primary production, etc.)?	→ **If yes:** it may qualify as business real property, which can make related-party leasing workable if conditions are met and the arrangement remains arm's length (s109). → **If no:** proceed.
Do you want offshore diversification (international property)?	→ **If yes:** possible, but you must still comply with Australian SMSF rules (strategy, governance, recordkeeping) and local country laws (tax, title, withholding, property management). (Higher admin/compliance load.) → **If no:** proceed.
Are you planning construction/development and using borrowing?	→ **If yes:** development becomes high-complexity because SMSF borrowing must fit a Limited Recourse Borrowing Arrangement framework (see SIS Act ss67A–67B). These rules drive how the asset is acquired/held and what changes are allowed during the loan term.

Factors to Consider When Choosing a Property

Selecting the right property for your SMSF requires more than simply choosing the type of property. Several critical factors must be evaluated to make an informed investment decision.

1. Location

Location is one of the most important factors influencing rental demand, property value appreciation, and overall investment performance. Ideal locations include areas with strong economic growth, population increases, and infrastructure development.

Location	Expected Rental Yield	Capital Growth Potential
Metropolitan Areas	3%–5%	High
Regional Areas	5%–7%	Medium to High
Commercial Zones	6%–8%	Variable
Rural Areas	4%–6%	Low to Medium

Source: SQM Research

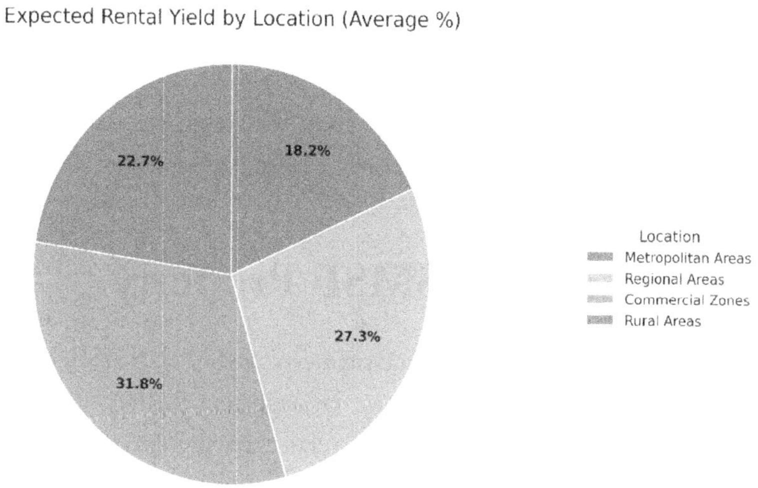

2. Rental Yield

Rental yield measures the annual rental income as a percentage of the property's value. Ensure the property generates enough rental income to cover loan repayments and property expenses, such as management fees, maintenance, and taxes.

3. Cash Flow Considerations

Positive cash flow is essential for SMSF investments. Cash flow covers loan repayments and property-related expenses, and ensures liquidity in the SMSF without needing to sell assets prematurely.

- **Loan Repayments:** Ensure the rental income is sufficient to cover repayments over time, especially considering potential interest rate fluctuations.
- **Super Contributions:** Factor in super contributions as part of the strategy to cover loan repayments.
- **Property Costs:** Include property management, maintenance, insurance, and taxes in your calculations.

4. Growth Potential

While rental yield is critical for short-term expenses, long-term wealth comes from capital growth. Look for areas with high population growth, employment opportunities, and infrastructure development, all of which drive demand and price appreciation.

How to Finance SMSF Property

There are two main ways to finance property within an SMSF: borrowing through a *Limited Recourse Borrowing Arrangement* (LRBA) using a traditional SMSF bank loan, or using a related party loan. A related party loan is usually funded by members of the fund using a line of credit or other personal funding to package into a related party loan, where they become the lender. The decision depends on your fund's liquidity and investment strategy.

Borrowing Through an LRBA

Borrowing through an LRBA allows an SMSF to purchase a more expensive property by leveraging its available capital. However, LRBAs come with strict lending criteria and require a larger deposit (typically 30%).

- **Advantages:** Allows for faster portfolio growth through leverage.
- **Disadvantages:** Higher interest rates and strict borrowing conditions reduce cash flow in the short term.

Financing Option	Key Features
LRBA	Leverage allows the SMSF to purchase higher-value properties. Higher interest rates (typically 1%–3% more than standard loans).
Cash Reserves	No debt burden, but limits purchasing power.

Using Personal Cash Reserves / Line of Credit Funding – Related Party Loan

A related party loan is when an SMSF borrows from a member, relative, or a related entity to acquire a single acquirable asset (usually property) under a *Limited Recourse Borrowing Arrangement* (LRBA). It is permitted if and only if the loan is on strictly arm's-length terms (e.g., interest rate, LVR, security, repayment schedule) consistent with the ATO's safe harbour guidance, properly documented with a written loan agreement and registered mortgage, and complies with the *SIS Act* LRBA rules (limited recourse to the asset) and Section 109 (arm's-length dealings).

Done correctly, it can solve bank finance hurdles and keep control "in-house"; done poorly (e.g., concessional rates, interest holidays, or inadequate security), it risks Non-Arm's-Length Income (NALI) tax at penalty rates, in-house asset breaches, or LRBA contraventions. In practice, trustees should evidence commerciality (rate benchmarking, amortisation, regular repayments), maintain independent valuations, and ensure all cash flows run through the SMSF's bank account to demonstrate genuine, market-standard lending.

Advantages: No bank approval process, easier and cheaper to set up.

Disadvantages: Higher interest rates and rates change annually.

Chapter 3 will address 'Related Party Loans' in more detail

SMSF Property: Repairs / Maintenance vs Improvements (ATO SMSFR 2012/1)

1. **Repairs/maintenance** can generally be funded with LRBA borrowings.
2. **Improvements** cannot be funded with LRBA borrowings.

Scenario	Repairs / Maintenance (allowed with LRBA borrowings)	Improvements (cannot be funded with LRBA borrowings)
1. Kitchen fire (residential)	Replace damaged cooktops, benches, walls, and ceilings with modern equivalents. Slightly better materials are OK if they don't significantly change the property overall. Adding a dishwasher = minor/trifling.	Extending the house to enlarge the kitchen. Adding a second "outdoor kitchen"/BBQ kitchen area – this is new functionality, functionality, not restoration.
2. General upkeep (gutters, paint)	Replace guttering and repaint. Add leaf guard to gutters = minor. Replace fence with modern equivalent; add a small access gate = minor. Install a smoke alarm to meet council rules.	Build a pergola/outdoor entertaining area. Add a pool or a new garage. Install whole-home automation/security / AV. Add an extra bathroom.
3. Roof damage (cyclone)	Replace the damaged roof with a modern equivalent. Better materials are OK if they don't significantly improve the overall asset beyond what it was.	Add a second storey at the same time as the roof works – that changes the scale/function of the dwelling.
4. Total loss in a fire	Rebuild a broadly comparable three-bedroom house. Using insurance proceeds is fine. Better-quality fittings are OK if overall it's still broadly comparable to what was destroyed.	Rebuild something not broadly comparable (substantially larger / different dwelling). This is treated as creating a different asset.
5. Outdated kitchen (wear and tear)	Renew an old but functional kitchen using modern equivalent materials and appliances, addressing wear and tear. Modernising without significantly upgrading the asset as a whole.	Demolish the existing house and rebuild something not broadly comparable. This is treated as creating a new asset.
6. Farm on a single title	Replace sections of existing cattle yards or fencing. Keep existing bores/windmills/tanks/troughs working. Replace failed pipes between an existing tank and trough.	Add a new set of cattle yards. Add an extra bore/windmill/tank/trough. Add a new dam, new shed, or ~2km of new fencing beyond the original. These are new additional assets.
7. Machinery under LRBA	Repair the hydraulic system right after purchase so the machine is restored to full working order.	Major overhaul where most significant parts are replaced, and performance is materially lifted. That's an upgrade, not a repair.

Compliance and Regulations

Before purchasing property through an SMSF, it is essential to ensure compliance with superannuation regulations. The key rules include:

- **Sole Purpose Test (SIS Act Section 62):** The property must be purchased solely to provide retirement benefits to the members of the SMSF.
- **Related Party Transactions (SIS Act Section 66):** SMSFs can only acquire certain properties from related parties, and all transactions must be conducted at market value.
- **Limited Recourse Borrowing (SIS Act Sections 67A & 67B):** SMSFs can borrow money to purchase property, but these arrangements must meet strict borrowing criteria to protect the other assets of the fund.
- **Arm's Length Rule (SIS Act Section 109):** All dealings involving SMSF property must be conducted on an arm's length basis, meaning transactions should reflect market rates.

Conclusion

Choosing the right property for your SMSF requires a careful balance between risk, return, and regulatory compliance. The types of properties available for investment through an SMSF provide flexibility, but they must be selected strategically to ensure alignment with your long-term financial goals. By understanding the available property types and the key factors influencing property investment, trustees can make informed decisions that maximise their SMSF's performance.

Reference Section for SIS Act Compliance

As requested, we will create a dedicated section later in the book to highlight the six key sections of the *SIS Act* that trustees must adhere to, ensuring complete compliance with the superannuation regulations:

1. **Sole Purpose Test** – *SIS Act* Section 62
2. **Related Party Rules** – *SIS Act* Section 66
3. **Borrowing Rules** – *SIS Act* Sections 67A & 67B
4. **In-House Asset Limits** – *SIS Act* Section 71
5. **Arm's Length Transactions** – *SIS Act* Section 109

These references will be crucial for trustees to understand their obligations and avoid penalties.

CHAPTER 3: SMSF Property Financing – LRBAs, Related Party Loans

Overview of SMSF Property Financing Options

Over the past decade, SMSF trustees have gained more tools beyond simply buying properties with cash or using traditional borrowing. Today, financing strategies range from conventional bank loans to creative approaches involving family members' funds or even cryptocurrency collateral. These innovations enable trustees to leverage personal assets—like superannuation savings or digital currencies—to increase their investment capacity while still meeting the strict requirements of superannuation law.

To set the stage, consider the key differences among the three main approaches. A Limited Recourse Borrowing Arrangement (LRBA) with a commercial lender typically requires a large deposit (often 30–40%) and charges high interest (roughly 7.5–9.5% p.a.) – reflecting its established, structured process. A Related-Party Loan (where a member lends to the SMSF) can offer competitive rates and flexibility but requires careful compliance with the ATO's safe harbour rules.

The table below summarises how these options compare in terms of rates, deposits, benefits, and risks:

Financing Method	Interest Rate	Deposit Required	Key Benefits	Primary Risks
Limited Recourse Borrowing (LRBA)	7.5–9.5% p.a. (approximately 2%–4% above standard home loans)	30–40% of property value	Established process, professional lenders	Higher interest rates, limited recovery if default
Related Party Loan (Member → SMSF)	8.95% p.a. (ATO safe harbour rate for 2025–26)	Flexible (member's funds)	Lower nominal rate than the bank, family control	Complex compliance, risk of NALI if undercharged

Each option has its place depending on the fund's resources and goals. The next sections dive into the details of each approach, including examples to illustrate how they work in practice.

Limited Recourse Borrowing Arrangements (LRBAs)

LRBA Fundamentals and Current Market

LRBAs remain the most common way for SMSFs to borrow for property. The *SIS Act* (Sections 67A–67B) allows an SMSF to take out a loan if strict rules are met. In an LRBA, the loan is secured only by the purchased asset (the "limited recourse" part), protecting other fund assets from creditor claims. The borrowed money must buy one single asset—no pooling multiple properties or buying businesses with the loan.

Importantly, any improvements to the property cannot be funded by borrowed money (the "asset replacement" rule). Finally, all terms of the loan (interest rate, fees, repayments) must be on commercial, arm's-length terms as if the parties were unrelated.

LRBA Overview	**Typical Features**
Deposit Required	30% of the property's purchase price
Interest Rates	1%–3% higher than traditional loans
Borrowing Restrictions	Funds must only be used to acquire a single property; no improvements or developments with borrowed money (**SIS Act Sections 67A & 67B**)
Repayment Source	Rental income, super contributions, or other income generated by the SMSF

In practice, lenders view SMSFs as higher risk than personal borrowers, so they set higher hurdles. As of 2024–25, expect interest rates around 7.5–9.5% p.a. for an SMSF housing loan, which is typically 2–4% above a normal investor mortgage. Lenders generally cap the Loan-to-Value Ratio (LVR) at 70% (some will allow 80% in special cases). This means the SMSF needs a deposit of 30–40% of the purchase price. Loan terms are usually 15–30 years, and the SMSF makes principal-and-interest repayments. These conditions reflect the extra risk and complexity: while the structure is well-established, it comes at a higher cost than a regular home loan.

Key LRBA features include the limited recourse clause (the lender can only seize the purchased property if the SMSF defaults), the single asset rule (loan used for one identifiable asset), the asset replacement restriction (no significant improvements with the borrowed funds), and strict arm's-length compliance (rates and fees must match the market). To set up an LRBA, an SMSF trustee usually engages a lender and a lawyer. Typical costs and fees are outlined below.

Cost Category	Amount Range	Frequency	Description
Establishment fees	\$600–\$1,500	One-time	Lender processing and setup fees
Legal documentation	\$1,500–\$3,000	One-time	Drafting loan agreements and mortgage docs
Property valuation	\$300–\$800	Setup + every 3–5 years	Independent market valuation
Annual loan fees	\$300–\$600	Annual	Lender's ongoing administration fees

These figures are indicative; exact fees vary by lender and adviser. For example, a trustee might pay around \$3,000 up-front for legal and setup costs, plus \$500 annually in loan servicing fees.

To illustrate, imagine an SMSF is buying a \$600,000 rental property. The trustees negotiate a 70% LVR loan with a bank, borrowing \$420,000 and using \$180,000 of SMSF cash as the deposit. If the interest rate is 8.5%, the loan's annual interest is about \$35,700. Over 25 years (principal + interest), this equates to roughly \$3,274 per month in payments.

To afford this, the property must generate sufficient income. For instance, a rent of \$32,000 per year (about a 5.3% yield on \$600,000) would be needed to cover the repayments and expenses. In a real fund, trustees would also budget for repairs, insurance, and management fees. If rent is lower, the great thing in SMSFs is the ability to use concessional contributions, usually paid by an employer into an SMSF, which can be used to meet any shortfalls or loan repayments. This makes the investment viable, compared with buying property outside super, where often, investors would need to dip into their savings or income to fund any shortfalls.

Related Party Loans (Member → SMSF)

The Strategic Alternative to Traditional Borrowing

Another financing route is for SMSF members to lend directly to their fund. Under *SIS Act* Section 109 (the arm's length rule), a member (or their entity) can provide cash to the SMSF for a property purchase. When properly documented, this related-party loan can offer slightly lower rates and flexibility compared to a bank, while keeping the interest payments within the family. However, to comply with the law, the loan must mimic a commercial deal: it needs a formal loan agreement, regular repayments, and an interest rate at or above the ATO's safe harbour benchmark.

ATO Safe Harbour Rate Framework

The cornerstone of a compliant related-party loan is using at least the safe harbour interest rate. This rate is updated annually (based on the RBA's announced variable housing loan rates) and represents the minimum "market" rate for SMSF loans. For the 2025–26 financial year, the safe harbour is 8.95% p.a. for real property loans. Charging this rate (or higher) ensures the loan meets arm's length standards. If the SMSF charges less, the difference can trigger the *Non-Arm's Length Income* (NALI) rules, potentially penalising the fund.

Trustees should incorporate an annual rate review process. Each May/June, when the RBA publishes new indicator rates, check if the safe harbour has changed and update the loan accordingly. This typically involves:

- Amending the loan agreement to reflect the new rate.
- Adjusting the repayment schedule (amortisation table) so payments align with the new rate.
- Recording the change in trustee minutes (noting the rationale and confirming compliance).

Failing to do so risks taxation at the top marginal rate. For example, if the old 9.35% rate increases to 10% and the trustee neglects to update the loan, the SMSF may inadvertently under-charge interest and incur a penalty tax on the difference.

The table below outlines a sample annual compliance timeline:

Timeline	Action Required	Documentation	Compliance Risk
May/June (each year)	Review the newly announced ATO safe harbour rate	Revised loan agreement with updated rate	High – NALI if the rate is not updated
By July 1	Implement new rate in loan calculations; update repayment schedule	Updated amortisation schedule	High – must have evidence of applying rate
Trustee meeting	Document rate change, ensure arm's-length terms	Meeting minutes recording rate justification and trustee approval	Medium – governance records should reflect the decision

Related Party Loan Structure and Documentation

A proper related-party loan requires a solid paperwork trail. At a minimum, the SMSF needs:

- **Formal loan agreement:** Signed by the member (lender) and the SMSF (borrower). It should specify the loan amount, interest rate (e.g. 8.95% p.a.), term (max 15 years), repayment frequency (often monthly P&I), and default provisions.
- **Amortisation schedule:** A breakdown of each payment into principal and interest over the loan term, which is updated whenever the rate changes.
- **Trustee minutes:** Minutes of the trustee meeting approving the loan terms. This should state that the trustee considered the loan arm's length, and that the rate is at least the ATO's safe harbour rate.
- **Security documentation:** If the loan is secured by the SMSF property (as it should be), the trustees must register the mortgage. If the lender is an associate of the member, a PPSR (*Personal Property Securities Register*) registration might be needed to perfect security over any assets.
- **Valuations and evidence:** Independent property valuations ensure the loan is not over-valued against the security, and records of where the interest rate was sourced (e.g. a bank's rate sheet or RBA report) can support the arrangement.

Below is a summary of these documents and how often to update them:

Document	Key Elements	Update Frequency
Loan Agreement	Principal, interest rate (ATO safe harbour), term, repayments	Annual (if rate changes)
Repayment Schedule	Shows each payment's principal and interest components	Update whenever the rate changes
Trustee Minutes	Approval of loan, rate justification, arm's length evidence	At the loan setup and annually
Security Docs	Registered mortgage (and PPSR if needed)	One-time, but review if needed

Maintaining these records demonstrates to auditors or regulators that the loan was conducted properly.

Example: Member-to-SMSF Loan (Related Party Loan)

To see the numbers clearly, let us consider a practical example.

Suppose a member lends their SMSF $200,000 at the 2024–25 ATO safe harbour rate of 8.95% p.a. over 15 years, with repayments of principal and interest (P&I) each month.

At this rate and term, the monthly repayment works out to approximately $2,073. Over the first year, the SMSF would pay roughly $17,900 in interest to the member. This interest counts as taxable income for the member, while the SMSF can deduct the interest expense, since it is a genuine commercial cost.

Over five years, the total interest paid would be about $104,800. For comparison, if the SMSF had borrowed the same $200,000 from a bank at 8.50% p.a., the monthly repayment would be approximately $2,019, and the total interest over five years would be about $101,000. In other words, the related-party loan costs around $3,800 more in total interest over five years, roughly $54 extra per month.

This cost difference is often acceptable to many SMSF trustees who value keeping the interest "in the family," avoiding the lengthy, expensive, and hard loan application processes, and maintaining flexibility with repayments. Noting that you need equity in other assets or savings to draw against to create or setup a related party loan.

Comparison: Related Party vs Bank LRBA Loan

Financing Method	Interest Rate	Monthly Payment	5-Year Interest Cost
LRBA (Commercial Bank Loan)	8.50% p.a.	$2,019	$101,000
Related Party Loan (Safe Harbour rate 2025-26)	8.95% p.a.	$2,073	$104,800
Difference	+0.45%	+$54/month	+$3,800 (approx.)

Key Takeaway

While the related-party loan is slightly more expensive on paper, it offers several practical benefits for SMSF trustees:

- **Control:** The member sets the loan terms within ATO safe harbour limits.
- **Simplicity:** No bank approval, mortgage insurance, or red tape.
- **Internal Returns:** Interest payments stay within the family group.
- **Flexibility:** The arrangement can often be adjusted more easily than commercial loans.

Financing Strategy Selection Framework

Choosing the right financing method depends on the SMSF's situation:

- **LRBA – Best for:** Funds with limited cash reserves that need a large loan. Trustees who are comfortable with a traditional lending process often pick LRBAs, especially when the property price is high (e.g. $300,000), and the extra deposit required is available. The clear legal framework of LRBAs makes them a "known quantity" for many professionals.
- **Related Party Loan – Best for:** Funds where members have substantial personal liquidity that they can lend. These loans offer competitive rates and give the family more control over the terms. They suit situations where preserving cash within the family is important, and the members can afford to tie up funds for the loan term.

No one method is universally "best." As a rough guide: an LRBA is a go-to when borrowing large sums traditionally; a related-party loan works when the family can self-fund.

Below is an example of how these strategies might be combined in a simple comparison for a $420,000 property:

Financing Strategy Comparison — $420,000 Property (2025–26)

To compare different SMSF financing strategies, let us consider a typical example where the fund purchases a property valued at $420,000. The SMSF contributes $100,000 (approximately 24%) from its own balance, with the remaining $320,000 (76%) financed through various lending arrangements.

The table below outlines the setup costs, annual interest, 5-year total cost, and complexity level under each approach.

Financing Comparison

Financing Strategy	Setup Costs	Annual Interest	5-Year Total Cost (Interest + Setup)	Complexity Level
LRBA (Bank) (e.g. $320,000 loan @ 8.5%)	$3,000	$27,200	$139,000	Medium
Related Party Loan (e.g. $320,000 loan @ 8.95% safe harbour)	$2,000	$28,640	$145,200	High

Scenario Explanation

In this scenario, the SMSF purchases the property for $420,000, using a *Limited Recourse Borrowing Arrangement* (LRBA) to borrow $320,000 over a 15-year term.

Bank LRBA (8.5%)

- The SMSF borrows from a commercial lender at 8.5% p.a.
- Monthly repayments are approximately $3,230, with total interest over five years of $136,000–$139,000.
- Setup costs (loan documentation, bare trust, lender fees) add around $3,000.

- **Complexity:** Medium, with moderate compliance obligations.

Related Party Loan (8.95%)

- The member lends to their SMSF under ATO safe harbour terms at 8.95% p.a., using a compliant LRBA structure.
- Monthly repayments are about $3,290, and the total 5-year interest is around $143,000–$145,000.
- The arrangement keeps interest "within the family" and offers control and flexibility but requires strong documentation.
- **Complexity:** High.

Assumptions and Notes

- All calculations are based on principal-and-interest (P&I) monthly repayments over 15 years.
- ATO Safe Harbour Rate for 2025–26: 8.95% p.a. (reviewed annually).
- Figures are rounded to the nearest hundred for clarity.
- Only the SMSF's costs are reflected — the member's separate crypto loan interest (where applicable) is excluded.
- Property acquisition costs (stamp duty, conveyancing, etc.) are excluded.

Advanced Combination Strategies

SMSF trustees are not limited to a single method; mixing techniques can optimise funding:

Hybrid Approach: For example, an SMSF might use $100k of its own cash, $100k from a related party loan, and $200k via an LRBA to buy a $400k property. In this case, the deposit is split among SMSF savings and family funds, reducing the total commercial loan needed. This can lower the fund's interest cost (since the bank loan is smaller) while still using the family's resources. The benefit is dual: the LRBA is smaller and maybe at a slightly lower rate, while the member loan covers part of the deposit at a known rate.

Example structure:

- SMSF cash reserves: $100,000 (25% of purchase)
- Related Party loan to SMSF: $100,000 (25%)
- LRBA from bank: $200,000 (50%)
  This diversified funding can be attractive, as it spreads risk and takes advantage of each source's strengths.

Sequential Property Development: Trustees building a portfolio might roll out financing in stages. For instance, the fund's first property could be financed with a related-party loan deposit and an LRBA. After accumulating equity and rental cash flow, the fund might tackle a second property. The deposit for the second could come from the fund's savings, plus additional member loans or even the Bitcoin-backed route if crypto assets are available. Each new mortgage further increases equity, which can then be leveraged again.

- Over time, the SMSF can layer LRBAs, member loans, and crypto lending to expand its holdings, always mindful of LVR limits and tax rules.

In any hybrid strategy, clear documentation for each component is essential, as each loan must stand on its own compliance footing.

Compliance Checklist

No matter which financing route is chosen, SMSF trustees must ensure all transactions comply with superannuation law. Key compliance checkpoints include:

Compliance Area	Requirement	Documentation/Evidence
Sole Purpose Test (SIS 62)	Asset must further retirement benefits	Investment strategy, trustee minutes
Arm's Length Rule (SIS 109)	Terms must match market rates	Independent valuations, market rate evidence
In-House Asset Limits (SIS 71)	Related-party assets ≤ 5% of fund value	Asset register, calculation worksheets
Investment Strategy (Reg 4.09A)	The strategy must allow the investment	Updated strategy document, meeting notes

For property investments, trustees typically show that the property suits the fund's retirement goals (sole purpose), that they paid market value (with a valuer's report), and that any related-party dealings (like loans or purchase of a member's property) stayed within the in-house asset cap. Regular reviews and detailed minutes, or strategy documents, are a must.

When it comes to related-party and Bitcoin-backed loans, additional diligence is needed:

- **Annual rate verification:** Keep a copy of the RBA/ATO notice or rate sheet that shows the safe harbour rate each year.
- **Market comparison:** Save evidence of similar loan terms (for example, a bank's loan schedule or an online lender quote) to prove the chosen rate is not below market.
- **Trustee governance:** File the meeting minutes where the trustees discussed and approved the loan rate. This shows deliberate decision-making.
- **Professional guidance:** If the arrangement is complex (especially with crypto), keep letters or reports from accountants or lawyers confirming the strategy.

In short, document everything. The quality of the documentation can make or break compliance: well-kept files and minutes provide a strong defense if the ATO ever reviews the loan.

Strategic Implementation Timeline

A structured plan ensures the chosen financing strategy is executed correctly. Here is an example 90-day timeline:

Month 1: Strategy Selection and Setup

- Analyse the SMSF's finances and members' situations to choose the best financing mix.
- Engage professional advisers (SMSF specialists, accountants, financial planners) to validate the plan.
- Prepare preliminary documents: draft the loan agreement framework and review the superannuation trust deed for borrowing power.
- Begin researching properties: narrow target areas, check market prices, and order initial valuations if needed.

Month 2: Documentation and Approvals

- Finalise the loan agreement with the member or lender, including interest rate and repayment terms.
- Register any required securities (e.g. lodge the mortgage at the land titles office, file a PPSR financing statement).
- Hold a trustee meeting to formally approve the loan terms and property acquisition; record all decisions and ensure compliance with the trust deed.
- If going the crypto route, set up the crypto loan (transfer collateral to the platform) and prepare the cash transfer to the SMSF.

Month 3: Implementation and Property Acquisition

- Draw down the loan funds (from the bank, member, or crypto platform) into the SMSF's account.
- Negotiate and sign the property purchase contract in the name of the SMSF's trustee company.
- Settle the property, paying the deposit and stamp duty from the SMSF's account.
- Arrange required insurance (landlord insurance, public liability) for the property before tenants move in.
- Establish ongoing processes: schedule annual loan reviews, rent collection, and accounting tasks. Ensure loan repayments commence smoothly according to the agreed schedule.

This phased approach gives trustees time to get guidance, prepare paperwork, and secure the property. Rushing steps—especially around compliance—can lead to mistakes, so sticking to a timeline helps keep everything on track.

Conclusion: Optimising SMSF Property Financing

The modern SMSF property finance landscape offers trustees more flexibility than ever. By understanding the features and trade-offs of LRBAs, related-party loans, and crypto-backed loans, trustees can choose a structure that matches their fund's cash flow, risk tolerance, and retirement goals. The ultimate aim is to grow the fund's property holdings in a way that is tax-efficient and compliant.

Compliance and Regulatory Obligations

Managing property within an SMSF requires strict adherence to superannuation regulations. The following key compliance areas must be observed:

- **Sole Purpose Test (SIS Act Section 62):** The property must be used solely for providing retirement benefits to the fund's members. Fund members and related parties cannot reside in or use the property unless it's a business leasing arrangement at market rates.
- **In-House Asset Rules (SIS Act Section 71):** SMSFs cannot hold more than 5% of their total assets in "in-house" assets, such as loans to related parties. This rule applies to properties leased to related businesses.
- **Arm's Length Transactions (SIS Act Section 109):** All transactions involving SMSF property must be conducted at arm's length. This means that the rental income, purchase price, and any other dealings must reflect market rates.

- **Limited Recourse Borrowing Arrangements (SIS Act Sections 67A & 67B):** Ensure that any borrowing arrangements comply with the strict rules governing LRBAs, particularly that borrowed funds cannot be used for property improvements beyond basic maintenance and repairs.

SMSF vs Personal Property Investment The Lifestyle Advantage

Overview

When an investor buys property personally, they do so with after-tax income; every repayment, rate rise, or vacancy hits their household budget directly. An SMSF, however, can use pre-tax super contributions and rental income to fund the same purchase. This structural difference is the reason SMSF property remains one of the most tax-efficient and lifestyle-preserving investment strategies available to Australian professionals.

Over time, based on a $420,000 property, using the 2025–26 ATO safe-harbour related-party loan rate of 8.95% annually, the projections below clearly demonstrate the benefits of SMSF property over personally held property, notwithstanding the negative gearing benefits of personal property for high-income earners.

Cash Flow and Tax Efficiency Explained

A personal property loan must be serviced entirely from take-home pay, which has already been taxed at the individual's marginal rate. An SMSF loan (LRBA), on the other hand, is funded by concessional super contributions (taxed at only 15%) and rental income, which is also taxed at just 15%.

For a professional earning $120,000 a year:

- $30,000 in annual super contributions (12% SG + salary sacrifice)
- Taxed at 15%, not 37%
- Saving roughly $6,600 per year in tax before even counting the property's rent.

Rental income within the SMSF is taxed at only 15%, while personal rent is taxed at up to 37%. Together, this creates a powerful cash-flow buffer that allows the SMSF to fund property without dipping into the investor's household budget.

10-Year Projected Cash Flow Comparison

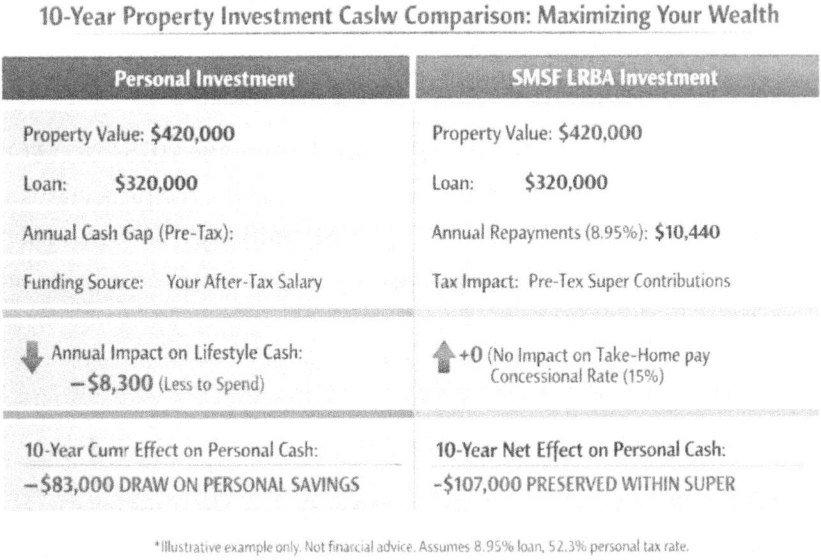

10-Year Property Investment Caslw Comparison: Maximizing Your Wealth

Personal Investment	SMSF LRBA Investment
Property Value: **$420,000**	Property Value: **$420,000**
Loan: **$320,000**	Loan: **$320,000**
Annual Cash Gap (Pre-Tax):	Annual Repayments (8.95%): **$10,440**
Funding Source: Your After-Tax Salary	Tax Impact: Pre-Tex Super Contributions
Annual Impact on Lifestyle Cash: **–$8,300** (Less to Spend)	**+0** (No Impact on Take-Home pay Concessional Rate (15%)
10-Year Cumr Effect on Personal Cash: –$83,000 DRAW ON PERSONAL SAVINGS	**10-Year Net Effect on Personal Cash:** -$107,000 PRESERVED WITHIN SUPER

*Illustrative example only. Not finaccial advice. Assumes 8.95% loan, 52.3% personal tax rate.

Result:

Over 10 years, the SMSF investor preserves roughly $190,000 in personal liquidity and enjoys a smoother lifestyle trajectory, all without reducing take-home pay.

10-Year Tax Efficiency Projection

Tax Element	SMSF (15%)	Personal (37%)	Cumulative 10-Year Difference
Rental Income Tax	$3,340 × 10 = $33,400	$8,240 × 10 = $82,400	$49,000 saved
Contributions Tax	$4,500 × 10 = $45,000	$11,100 × 10 = $111,000	$66,000 saved
Total Tax Paid (10 yrs)	$78,400	$193,400	$115,000 lifetime tax advantage

The Takeaway

The SMSF structure effectively turns every dollar of super contributions and rent into an accelerated debt-repayment engine, operating in a low-tax environment.

This means:

- More income stays invested within the fund.
- The property loan is paid down faster.
- Members keep their household income intact.

Over time, this translates into a compounding lifestyle advantage, growing retirement wealth inside super while maintaining lifestyle freedom outside it.

Lifestyle and Risk Insights

- **Lifestyle protection:** All repayments are made inside super, preserving household income.
- **Tax insulation:** The 15% environment smooths volatility and protects against interest-rate rises.
- **Diversification:** SMSF assets include cash, shares, and property, offering natural buffers if rent falls.
- **Retirement readiness:** The property becomes a tax-free asset once in the pension phase.

In plain terms, SMSF investors grow retirement wealth while still living comfortably now. Personal investors fund the same property but sacrifice lifestyle, cash flow, and flexibility.

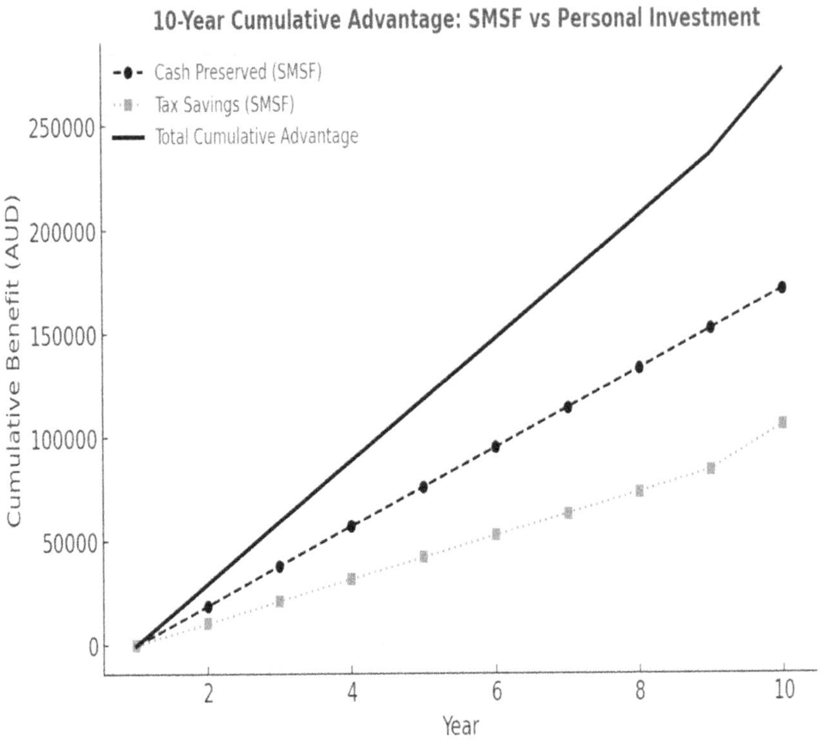
10-Year Cumulative Advantage: SMSF vs Personal Investment
Cash Preserved (SMSF)
Tax Savings (SMSF)
Total Cumulative Advantage
Cumulative Benefit (AUD)
250000
200000
150000
100000
50000
0
2
4
6
8
10
Year

Strategic Takeaway

SMSF Property Advantages

- Uses pre-tax money for repayments.
- Pays lower tax on income and gains.
- Preserves personal lifestyle and savings capacity.
- Builds long-term wealth inside a protected structure.

Personal Property Limitations

- Uses after-tax income.
- Higher ongoing tax drag.
- Immediate pressure on personal budget.
- Reduced ability to invest elsewhere.

Conclusion

Over a 10-year horizon, the SMSF property strategy delivers:

- **$190,000+** in preserved cash flow.
- **$100,000+** in tax savings.
- **Zero impact** on lifestyle spending.

The Bottom Line

SMSF property investment allows trustees to build substantial wealth through property while preserving their personal lifestyle and financial flexibility, a combination that personal property investment simply cannot match.

This analysis reinforces why SMSF property investment has become such a powerful strategy for Australians seeking to enhance their retirement outcomes without compromising their current quality of life.

CHAPTER 4: Using Bitcoin to Buy Property in an SMSF

Diversifying from Cryptocurrency to Property

The rise of cryptocurrency, particularly Bitcoin, has introduced unique opportunities for SMSF trustees seeking portfolio diversification and wealth building. While Bitcoin offers significant growth potential, its volatility presents risks that many investors seek to balance with more stable assets.

This chapter explores how SMSF members can use their personal Bitcoin holdings – without selling and triggering Capital Gains Tax – to fund property acquisitions within their SMSF. This sophisticated strategy allows trustees to:

- Preserve Bitcoin exposure while accessing its value for property investment.
- Avoid Capital Gains Tax by not disposing of cryptocurrency.
- Diversify into property for stable, inflation-protected income.
- Leverage the tax-free pension phase and $1.9 million pension cap for maximum tax efficiency.

CRITICAL REQUIREMENT: This strategy requires the member to hold cryptocurrency personally, outside the SMSF. The crypto cannot be held within the SMSF for this structure to work.

Current Landscape: Cryptocurrency in Australian SMSFs

Market Growth and Adoption

The Australian SMSF cryptocurrency market has experienced exponential growth:

Year	Crypto Assets in SMSFs	Growth Rate
2019	$200 million	Base year
2020	$137 million	-31.5% (market correction)
2024	$1.0 billion	+630% from 2020
2025	$1.675 billion	+67.5% from 2024

As of March 2025, approximately $1.675 billion in crypto assets are held by Australian SMSFs. Nearly 4 million Australians held crypto in 2024, with almost one-third of Gen Z owning digital assets.

Regulatory Framework

SMSFs can legally invest in cryptocurrencies, but must meet strict regulatory requirements under the ATO and *SIS Act*:

Essential Compliance Requirements:

- **Trust Deed Modification:** Crypto must be explicitly included in the SMSF trust deed and investment strategy.
- **Asset Separation:** Cryptocurrencies must be held in accounts registered in the SMSF's name, not individual trustees.
- **Approved Platforms:** Transactions must occur through regulated, AUSTRAC-registered exchanges only.
- **Documentation:** Comprehensive records including wallet addresses, transaction IDs, and valuations.
- **Prohibited Transactions:** Cannot acquire crypto from related parties or transfer personal holdings into the fund.

The Bitcoin-Backed Property Strategy

Core Strategy Overview

This advanced method allows SMSF trustees to access their personal cryptocurrency wealth for property investment without selling it:

1. Member pledges **personal** Bitcoin to a crypto lending platform.
2. The Platform provides AUD cash loan (no CGT event – no disposal occurred).
3. Member lends cash to their SMSF under a formal Related Party Loan agreement.
4. SMSF uses funds as a property deposit, combining with existing savings.
5. Property is acquired in SMSF, generating rental income.
6. SMSF repays members using rental income (tax-deductible to the SMSF).
7. Member services external crypto loan with SMSF payments.

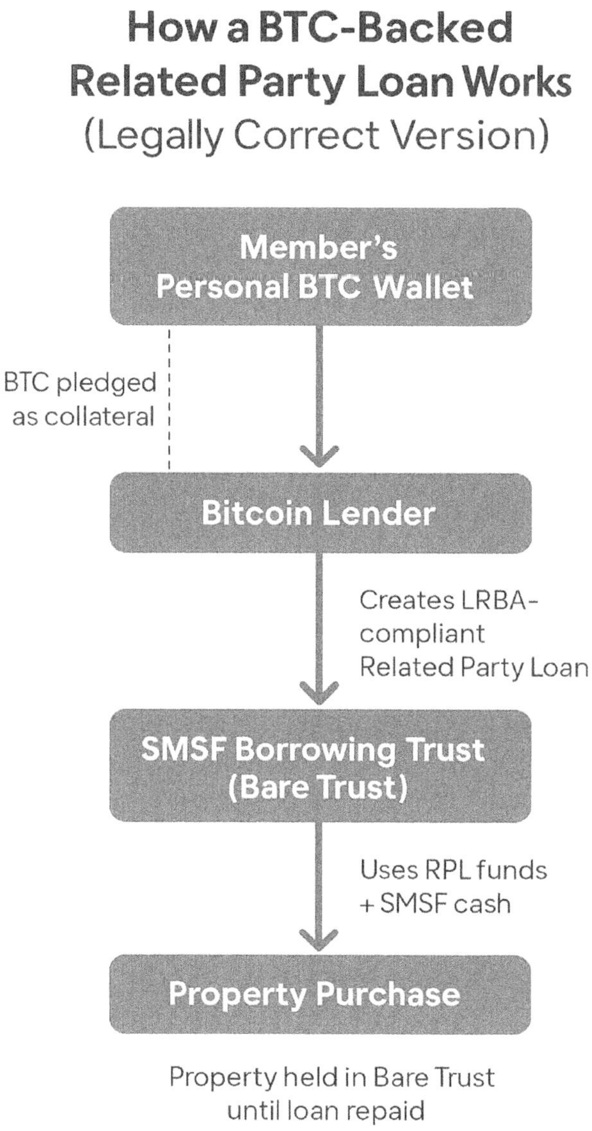
How a BTC-Backed
Related Party Loan Works
(Legally Correct Version)
Member's
Personal BTC Wallet
BTC pledged
as collateral
Bitcoin Lender
Creates LRBA-
compliant
Related Party Loan
SMSF Borrowing Trust
(Bare Trust)
Uses RPL funds
+ SMSF cash
Property Purchase
Property held in Bare Trust
until loan repaid

Key Benefits / Tax Benefits:

Member Key Benefits / Tax Benefits:

- **No CGT Event:** Member keeps cryptocurrency intact, and gains remain unrealised and tax-free.
- **Asset Retention:** Maintain Bitcoin ownership and potential appreciation.
- **Tax Deductions:** SMSF deducts loan interest payments, reducing taxable income.
- **Pension Phase Potential:** Future tax-free property gains and rental income.

Financial Benefits:

- **SMSF Funding:** Access deposit capital otherwise unavailable.
- **Dual Asset Exposure:** Benefit from both Bitcoin appreciation and property growth.
- **Inflation Protection:** Property provides stable, inflation-adjusted income.
- **Leverage Optimization:** Access the property market while maintaining crypto upside.

Important Note: This strategy is complex and involves costs (crypto loan interest). It suits only those comfortable with digital assets and intricate structuring.

Bitcoin Lending Platforms

Block Earner (Australia)

Block Earner launched Australia's first Bitcoin-backed home loans in July 2025 after winning a Federal Court case against ASIC:

Feature	Specification
Loan Currency	AUD
Interest Rate	~9.5% p.a.
Origination Fee	2% of loan amount
Max LVR	50-60%
Loan Purpose	Home loans/property deposits
Custody	Fireblocks (institutional grade)
Loan Term	Up to 4 years interest-only
Early Repayment	No penalties
Market Experience	7+ years established

Key Features:

- AUD-denominated loans (no currency risk).
- 30-day notice for margin calls at 60% LVR.
- Over $110 million in early borrower interest.
- Australian-based support and regulation.

Ledn (Global)

Ledn offers secure Bitcoin-backed loans globally with an established track record:

Feature	Specification
Loan Currency	USD (can fund in AUD)
Interest Rate	11.4% annual (13.4% APR)
Fee	$0 - No origination fee
Max LVR	50%
Minimum Collateral	$1,000 USD
Loan Term	12 months
Repayment	No monthly payments required
Early Repayment	No penalties
Market Experience	7+ years established

Feature, Specification | Loan Feature, AUD 30%

Key Features:

- 24-hour funding after collateral submission.
- BitGo custody (institutional grade).
- Hypothecated and non-hypothecated options.
- Global platform with a proven track record.

Platform Comparison

Platform Comparison

Criteria	Block Earner	Ledn
Geographic Focus	Australia	Global
Currency	AUD	USD
Interest Rate	9.5% p.a.	11.4% p.a.
Fee	2% ($6,720 on $336k)	$0
Loan Term	4 years interest-only	12 months flexible
Currency Risk	None	Yes (USD/AUD)
Status	Confirmed	Established
Custody	Fireblocks	BitGo
Loan Term	4 years interest-only	12 months flexible
Currency Risk	None	Yes (USD/AUD)
Status	Confirmed	Established
Custody	Fireblocks	BitGo

Platform Selection Considerations:

- **Block Earner:** Lower ongoing rate, AUD currency, but 2% upfront fee.
- **Ledn:** No upfront fee, established track record, but higher rate and USD risk.
- **Cost Example (Year 1):** Block Earner = $22,680 total ($16k interest + $6,720 fee) vs Ledn = $38,304 (interest only).
- **Strategy:** Consider splitting Bitcoin between both platforms for risk diversification.

Important: Trustees must verify current rates and legal status before selecting any platform.

The Complete Structure: How It Works

Three-Loan Architecture

This strategy operates through three distinct components that must remain separate:

Component 1: Personal Bitcoin Collateral

- Member owns 6 Bitcoin personally ($672,000 at $112,000 each).
- Held outside SMSF in personal name.
- Remains the member's property throughout.

Component 2: External Crypto Loan (Personal)

- Member borrows $336,000 from Block Earner/Ledn.
- 50% LVR provides volatility buffer.
- Bitcoin held in institutional custody (Fireblocks/BitGo).
- Interest rate: 9.5-11.4% p.a.
- No CGT event (no disposal of Bitcoin).
- Sits entirely outside *SIS Act* framework.

Component 3: Related Party LRBA (SMSF)

- Member lends $336,000 to their SMSF.
- Interest rate: 8.95% p.a. (ATO safe harbour 2025-26).
- Term: 15 years, monthly P&I payments.
- First mortgage over SMSF property.

- Complies with *SIS Act* s.67A-B, s.109.

Critical Separation: The SMSF interacts only with the member, never with the crypto platform. Each loan must stand alone.

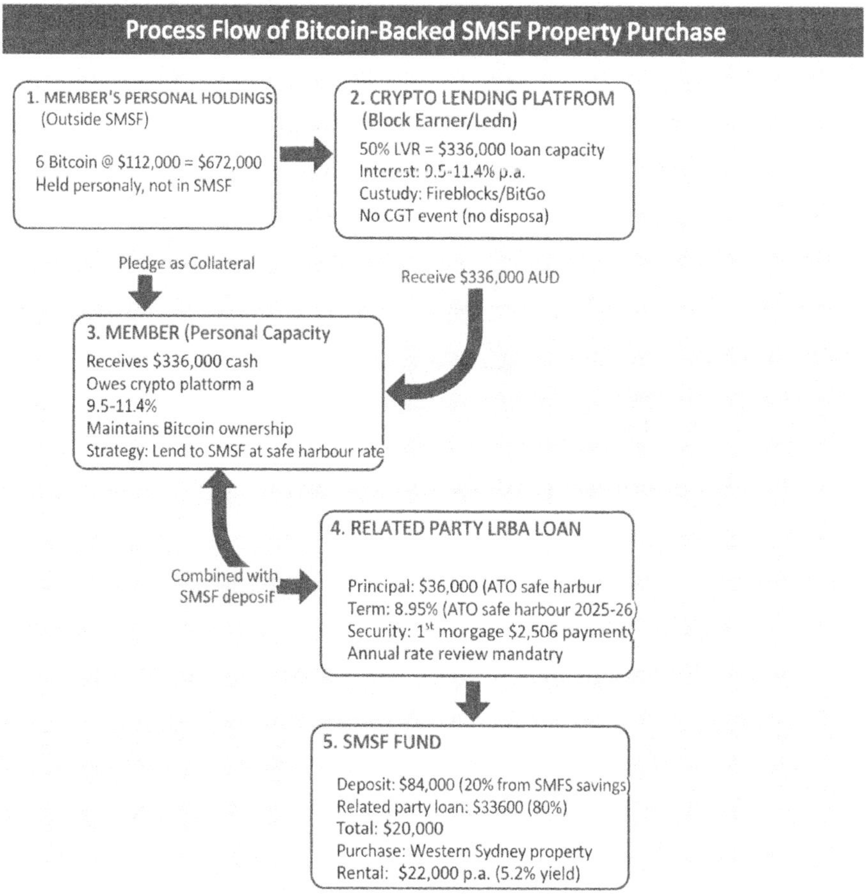

How Repayments Flow

How Repayments Flow

Flow	Direction	Amount (Annual)	Purpose
Crypto Loan	Platform → - Member	$336,000	One-time disbursement
SMSF Loan	Member → - SMSF	$336,000	One-time disbursement
SMSF Payments	SMSF → - Member	$30,072	8.95% interest + principal
Crypto Payments	Member → - Platform	$38,136	11.4% interest (Ledn example)
Funding Gap	Member's cost	$8,064	Net annual cost (2.4%)

Three-Year Analysis:

- **Total funding gap:** $24,192 over 3 years.
- **Bitcoin appreciation (10% p.a.):** $672,000 → $895,000 = $223,000 gain.
- The funding gap is easily covered by Bitcoin appreciation.
- **Alternative:** Repay crypto loan Year 2-3 using Bitcoin gains.

Detailed Implementation Example

Scenario Summary: Western Sydney Property

Property Details

Property Value:	**$420,000** (Western Sydney unit)
Location	Growth corridor, strong rental demand
Expected Yield	5.2% ($22,000 p.a.)

SMSF Funding

SMSF Deposit (20%)	**$84,000** (from existing SMSF savings of $150,000)
Related Party Loan	**$336,000**

Bitcoin Collateral

Bitcoin Required	6 BTC @ $112,000 each = $672,000
Platform LVR	50% ($336,000 on $672,000 collateral)

Loan Terms

SMSF Loan Rate	8.95% p.a. (ATO safe harbour 2025-26)

External Crypto Loan

Crypto Loan Rate	11.35% p.a. (Ledn example)
Annual Crypto Interest	$38,136

Loan Terms

SMSF Loan Rate	8.95% p.a. (ATO safe harbour 2025-26)
SMSF Loan Term	15 years
Monthly SMSF Payment	$2,506 (Principal & Interest)
Annual SMSF Payment	$30,072

Funding Gap

Annual Cost to Member	$8,064 (2.4% differential)
Three-Year Total	$24,192

Process Flow of Bitcoin-Backed SMSF Property Purchase

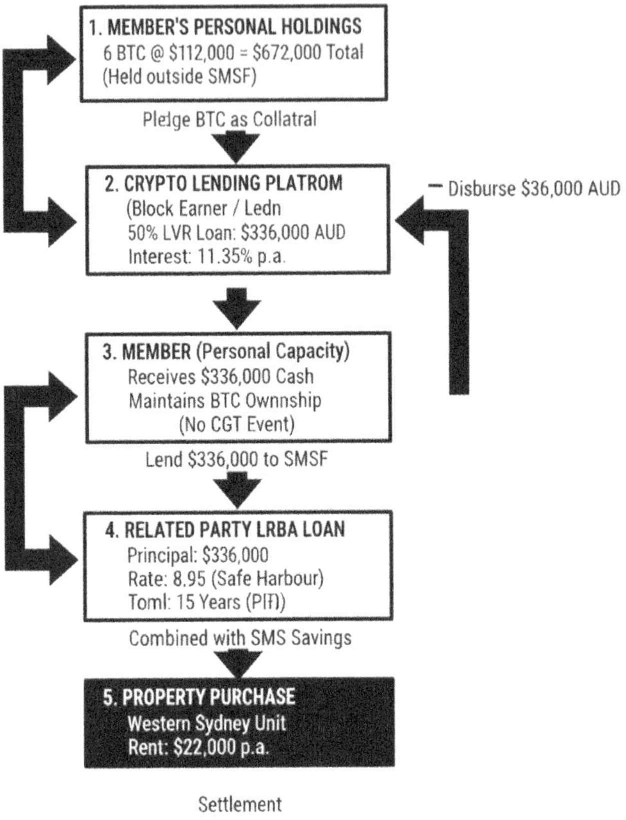

Financial Projections: 5-Year Outlook

Year	Bitcoin Value*	Property Value**	SMSF Loan Balance	Net Wealth
Year 1	$739,200	$441,000	$329,280	$851,920
Year 2	$813,120	$463,050	$322,176	$953,994
Year 3*	$894,432	$486,203	$314,659	$1,065,976
Year 4	$983,875	$510,513	$306,707	$1,187,681
Year 5	$1,082,263	$536,038	$298,296	$1,320,005

Year 1	*5% annual growth forecast
Year 3	**5% annual growth forecast

*5% annual growth forecast

**Assumes 10% annual Bitcoin appreciation*
***Assumes 5% annual property appreciation*
****Crypto loan repaid by Year 3 using Bitcoin appreciation*

Key Observations:

- Bitcoin grows from $672,000 to $1,082,000 (61% increase over 5 years).
- Property grows from $420,000 to $536,000 (28% increase).
- SMSF loan reduces from $336,000 to $298,000.
- Net wealth increases by $648,005 (102% return on initial $672,000 Bitcoin position).

- Funding gap ($24,192 over 3 years) easily offset by $223,000 Bitcoin gain.

ATO Safe Harbour Compliance: Critical Requirements

Understanding Safe Harbour Rates

The ATO publishes annual safe harbour interest rates for related party loans to SMSFs. Using these rates provides protection from Non-Arm's Length Income (NALI) taxation.

Current Rates (2025-26):

- **Real Property:** 8.95% p.a. (down from 9.35% in 2024-25)
- **Listed Securities:** 10.95% p.a. (down from 11.35% in 2024-25)
- **Publication:** Announced each May by RBA
- **Implementation:** Must be applied from July 1 each year

Historical Rate Changes:

Financial Year	Real Property	Change from Prior Year
2025-26	8.95%	**-0.40%** (decrease)
2024-25	9.35%	**+0.50%** (increase)
2023-24	8.85%	**+3.50%** (large increase)
2022-23	5.35%	**+0.25%** (increase)
2021-22	5.10%	Base comparison

Critical Observations:

- Rates fluctuate annually based on economic conditions.
- 2023-24 saw largest increase (+3.50%) during a rising interest rate environment.
- 2025-26 shows first decrease (-0.40%).
- Annual volatility requires careful cash flow planning.

Why Safe Harbour Rates Are Mandatory

Compliance Protection:

- Using a safe harbour rate provides certainty of arm's length treatment.
- Protects against ATO challenge of the loan terms.
- Prevents NALI taxation at 45%.

Non-Compliance Consequences:

- **Below Safe Harbour:** NALI taxation at 45% on ALL SMSF income (not just difference).
- **Poor Documentation:** ATO may challenge the entire loan arrangement.
- **Missing Annual Reviews:** Compliance failures and penalties.
- **Permanent Impact:** Once NALI is triggered, it cannot be reversed.

Annual ATO Safe Harbour Rate Review

Each year, the safe harbour rate review follows a fixed cadence. In late May, the RBA releases its Indicator Lending Rates; SMSF trustee/members should monitor the RBA site and capture the relevant page for the file. In early June, the ATO publishes the new safe harbour rates; at that point, notify your SMSF accountant and begin the documentation process.

By mid to late June, recalculate the new monthly repayment, prepare an updated amortisation schedule, draft and sign trustee minutes approving adoption of the new rate, and compile the rate justification evidence (RBA and ATO printouts).

On 1 July, the new rate becomes effective: the first repayment at the updated amount is due, the updated documents are filed to the audit pack, and the member is notified of the revised payment.

The annual evidence pack should include: the RBA announcement, the ATO safe harbour confirmation, the new repayment schedule, signed trustee minutes (recording the rate adoption, term continuation, and compliance confirmation), an updated loan agreement schedule (addendum), the member notification letter, and the accounting system update confirmations.

Growth of Property V Bitcoin:

Year	Property Value (5% growth)	BTC Portfolio Value (25% growth)	Total Asset Position
Year 0	$420,000	$672,000	**$1,092,000**
Year 3	$486,200	$1,312,500	**$1,798,700**
Year 5	$536,000	$2,050,700	**$2,586,700**
Year 10	**$684,100**	**$6,258,600**	**$6,942,700**

Comprehensive Documentation Requirements

Essential Documents Checklist

Document	Key Requirements	Annual Updates	Risk Level
Loan Agreement	• 8.95% safe harbour rate • 15-year term • Monthly P&I $2,506	• Annual rate adjustment: • Updated schedule	CRITICAL NALI if incorrect
Repayment Schedule	• Payment amounts • Principal/interest split	• Monthly (tracking) • Annual reconciliation	HIGH Audit evidence
Trustee Minutes	• Loan approval rationale • Rate justification • Best interests assessment	• Annual rate review (Strategy alignment)	CRITICAL Regulatory evidence
Security Documentation	• Mortgage registration • PPSR registration • Property valuation	• Annual valuation • Insurance renewals	MEDIUM Asset protection
Payment Records	• Bank transfers • Payment reconciliation	• Monthly tracking • Annual reconciliation	HIGH Audit trail
ATO Rate Evidence	• New rate documentation (May) • Implementation evidence (July)	• New rate documentation (May)	CRITICAL NALI avoidance
Investment Strategy	• Property acquisition rationale • Loan strategy justification	• Annual review and update	MEDIUM Sole purpose test
Tenant Agreements	• Arm's length terms • Market rent evidence • No related parties	• Lease renewals • Rent reviews	HIGH Related party rules

CRITICAL NALI avoidance MEDIUM Sole purpose test HIGH Related party rules

Loan Agreement Must Include

Essential Clauses:

1. **Parties:** Member (lender) and SMSF trustee (borrower).
2. **Principal amount:** $336,000.
3. **Interest rate:** 8.95% p.a. (current ATO safe harbour).
4. **Annual rate review clause** (references ATO safe harbour).
5. **Term:** 15 years from commencement date.

6. **Repayment:** Monthly principal and interest ($2,506).
7. **Security:** First registered mortgage over SMSF property.
8. **Default provisions:** Standard commercial terms.
9. **Early repayment:** Allowed without penalty.
10. **Compliance statements:** References to *SIS Act* and *PCG 2016/5*.

Common Mistakes to Avoid:

❌ Using outdated safe harbour rates
❌ Missing annual review clause
❌ Inadequate security documentation
❌ Interest-only terms (must be P&I)
❌ Terms exceeding 15 years for property
❌ Missing default provisions
❌ Informal or handshake agreements
❌ No trustee minutes

SIS Act Compliance Framework

Legal Requirements Summary

Requirement	Condition	Legal Reference	Compliance Action
Borrowing	An SMSF may borrow only under LRBA	SIS Act s.67A-B	Structure as bare trust, limited recourse
Related Party Lender	Loan from a member permitted	SIS Act s.109	Formal loan agreement required
Interest Rate	Must be commercial/ arm's length	ATO PCG 2016/5	Use **8.95%** safe harbour rate (2025-26)
Loan Term	Maximum 15 years for property	ATO PCG 2016/5	Document 15-year term
Repayment	Must be principal & interest	ATO PCG 2016/5	No interest-only permitted
Security	Limited to property only	SIS Act s.67A(1)(a)(ii)	No recourse to other SMSF assets
In-House Asset	Related party loan normally prohibited	SIS Act s.71(8)	LRBA exemption applies
Bitcoin Collateral	Must be held outside SMSE	SIS Act s.62 (Sole Purpose)	Member's personal holdings only
Annual Review	Rate must be updated annually	ATO PCG 2016/5	Review by July 1 each year
Investment Strategy	Property acquisition	SIS Act s.71(8)	LRBA exemption applies
Bitcoin Collateral	Must be held outside SMSF	SIS Act s.62 (Sole Purpose)	Member's personal holdings only
Annual Review	Rate must be updated annually	ATO PCG 2016/5	Review by July 1 each year

Permitted vs Prohibited Actions

PERMITTED:

SMSF Actions:

- Use rental income to repay the related party loan.
- Use member contributions to service loan.
- Claim tax deduction for interest payments (15% in accumulation, 0% in pension).
- Make regular scheduled payments to member.
- Adjust payment amounts annually for rate changes.
- Hold property in a bare trust structure.

Member Actions:

- Pledge personal Bitcoin as external collateral.
- Borrow from a crypto platform personally.
- Lend proceeds to SMSF at safe harbour rate.
- Receive interest and principal from SMSF.
- Declare SMSF interest as personal income.
- Use SMSF payments to service a crypto loan.

🚫 PROHIBITED:

SMSF Cannot:

- Pay or guarantee member's external crypto loan (s.65 breach).
- Hold Bitcoin directly as loan collateral.
- Accept related party as tenant (sole purpose breach).
- Use interest rate below safe harbour (triggers NALI).
- Skip annual rate review and adjustment.
- Use interest-only repayments.
- Extend loan term beyond 15 years for property.
- Provide financial assistance to a member for a crypto loan.

Member Cannot:

- Transfer personal Bitcoin into SMSF as collateral.
- Charge SMSF above-market commercial rate.
- Rent SMSF property for personal use.
- Use SMSF funds for personal expenses.
- Avoid declaring SMSF interest as personal income.
- Combine SMSF and crypto loan repayments.

Tax Implications and Strategic Outcomes

CGT Treatment Comparison

Strategy	CGT Triggered	Tax Implications	Asset Retention	Net Benefit
Sell Bitcoin, Buy Property	✓ Yes	Full CGT at marginal rate (e.g. 23.5%)	⊗ No Bitcoin	Low - Tax erosion
Bitcoin-Backed Loan	✗ No	No disposal, no CGT	✓ Yes	High - No tax, retain Bitcoin
Hold Bitcoin Only	✗ No	No current tax	✓ Yes	Medium - No diversification
Repayment	✗ No	Must be principal & interest	✓ No interest-only permitted	
Security	✓ Yes	No disposal, no CGT	✓ No recourse to other SMSF assets	High - No tax, retain Bitcoin
In-House Asset	✗ No	No current tax	✓ Yes	Medium - No diversification
Bitcoin Collateral	✓ Yes	Must be held outside SMSF	✓ Member's personal holdings only	

Example Tax Impact on $400,000 Bitcoin Gain:

Scenario	Tax Treatment	Tax Paid	Net Proceeds
Sell in Personal Name	50% discount, 37% rate	$74,000	$326,000
Sell in SMSF (Accumulation)	33% discount, 15% rate	$40,000	$360,000
Sell in SMSF (Pension Phase)	0% tax (tax-free)	$0	$400,000
Bitcoin-Backed Loan	No disposal, no CGT	$0	$400,000 + retained Bitcoin

Combined Tax Effect:

Phase	Member Tax Cost	SMSF Tax Benefit	Net Tax Impact
Accumulation	-$11,127	+$4,511	-$6,616
Pension	-$11,127	$0	-$11,127

Strategic Outcome: Tax cost is modest compared to $223,000 Bitcoin appreciation over 3 years.

Pension Phase Strategy

The $1.9 million transfer balance cap (2024-25) provides powerful tax optimization opportunities:

Strategic Outcomes Over Time

Scenario	Effect on Member	Effect on SMSF	Wealth Impact
Bitcoin Appreciates 10% p.a.	BTC grows $672k → $1.08M. Crypto loan safer Can reduce LVR	Continues earning rent Building property equity Loan balance reducing	+$648k net wealth over 5 years
Property Appreciates 5% p.a.	Receives steady loan repayments. Consistent income stream	Property $420k → $536k Asset appreciation Inflation protection	+$116k property equity
Enter Pension Phase	Continues receiving payments Still taxable personally	Rental income tax-free Property gains tax-free Maximum efficiency	Save $4,500+ annually
Bitcoin Falls 30%	May need to add collateral Personal risk only		SMSF wealth preserved

Risk Management Framework

Comprehensive Risk Analysis

Cryptocurrency Volatility Risk

Risk Factor	Likelihood	Impact	Mitigation Strategy
Bitcoin -10 to -20%	High	Low	• Maintain 40-45% LVR buffer • Daily price monitoring • Price alerts at -15%
Bitcoin -20 to -40%	Medium	Medium	• 30-day margin call notice • Cash reserves for top-up • Consider partial loan repayment
Bitcoin -40% or more	Low	High	• Potential forced liquidation • SMSF fully protected • Member absorbs loss personally
Extreme Volatility	Medium	Medium	• Conservative initial LVR • Multiple platform diversification • Never exceed 50% LVR
Extreme Volatility	Medium	Medium	• Conservative initial LVR • Multiple platform diversification • Never exceed 50% LVR

NALI Prevention Checklist:

- ✅ Use current ATO safe harbour rate (8.95% for 2025-26)
- ✅ Update rate by July 1 each year
- ✅ Document rate review in trustee minutes
- ✅ Maintain written loan agreement
- ✅ Evidence arm's length terms
- ✅ Independent rate benchmarking
- ✅ Professional accountant oversight

Final Suggestions

Before Proceeding:

1. Verify Eligibility:

- Confirm Bitcoin is held personally (not in SMSF) non-negotiable.
- Check SMSF has deposit funds and allows borrowing.
- Assess personal capacity for a 3-year funding gap.
- Verify stable income and emergency reserves.
- Check Bitcoin lending platform risk

Conclusion

Investing in SMSF property using personally held Bitcoin via a related party loan or other cryptocurrency is a great way to diversify from a volatile asset such as Bitcoin to a conventional stable asset, like property, which can provide inflation-hedged rental income and steady capital values for SMSF members in the accumulation and pension phases. Using the $1.9 million pension balance cap per person is an effective way to sell an asset like property and Bitcoin and reduce sizable capital gains to benefit your retirement. By understanding the tax-free benefits of the super pension phase, trustees can maximise the value of both their cryptocurrency and property investments, ensuring a secure and diversified retirement portfolio.

The foundation you build today through careful implementation, professional guidance, and ongoing compliance will position you to benefit from the continued integration of digital assets and traditional investment markets.

Reference Section

1. **Capital Gains Tax (CGT) Discount:** One-third discount on Bitcoin held 12+ months, reducing CGT to 10% in the accumulation phase.
2. **$1.9 Million Pension Cap (2024-25):** Allows tax-free income and capital gains within this cap per person ($3.8M for couples).
3. **Limited Recourse Borrowing Arrangements (LRBAs):** Allows SMSFs to borrow for property purchases with limited recourse to a single asset.
4. **ATO Safe Harbour Rates (2025-26):**

- **Real Property:** 8.95% p.a. (down from 9.35% in 2024-25).
- **Listed Securities:** 10.95% p.a.
- Published annually each May, mandatory annually by July 1.

5. ***SIS Act* s.67A-B:** Governs SMSF borrowing arrangements and LRBA structures.
6. ***ATO PCG 2016/5*:** Practical Compliance Guideline for related party loans, safe harbour terms, and NALI avoidance.
7. **Block Earner:** Australian Bitcoin lending platform, AUD loans, ~9.5% p.a., 2% origination fee, Fireblocks custody, ASIC appeal pending.
8. **Ledn:** Global Bitcoin lending platform, USD/AUD loans, 11.4% p.a., $0 origination fee, BitGo custody, 7+ years established.
9. **NALI (Non-Arm's Length Income):** Income from non-commercial arrangements taxed at 45%, triggered by below-safe-harbour rates.
10. ***SIS Act* s.109:** Governs related party transactions, including member-to-SMSF loans.
11. **Property Inflation Hedge:** Rental income adjusts with inflation, preserving purchasing power in debt-laden markets.
12. **Pension Phase Tax Benefits:** 0% tax on income and capital gains within $1.9M cap per person.

Disclaimer

This chapter provides general information only and does not constitute financial, tax, or legal advice. The Bitcoin-backed SMSF property strategy is complex and involves significant risks, including:

- Cryptocurrency volatility (30-50% price swings possible).
- NALI taxation risk (45% tax if non-compliant).
- Platform counterparty risk (insolvency, custody breaches).
- Regulatory uncertainty (ASIC appeals, changing rules).
- Compliance burden (annual reviews mandatory).

All trustees must obtain professional advice from:

- Qualified SMSF specialist accountants.
- SMSF lawyers with Bitcoin experience.
- Licensed financial advisors.
- Independent property valuers.

Before implementing this strategy, past cryptocurrency performance does not indicate future results. Property values can decline. Interest rates can increase significantly. The strategy requires personal Bitcoin holdings outside the SMSF—SMSF-held crypto cannot be used.

Failure to comply with ATO safe harbour rates or annual review requirements will trigger permanent NALI taxation at 45% on all SMSF income. This cannot be reversed. Professional guidance is essential for compliance and success.

Always consult qualified professionals before proceeding.

CHAPTER 5: SMSF Property Investment Strategies: Business and International

Investing in real estate through a self-managed super fund (SMSF) offers powerful retirement-planning opportunities. SMSFs have been investing in business real property (commercial premises) longer than investment property, even international property, under strict conditions. These strategies let small business owners and retirees use their SMSFs to buy or transfer property, lease it back to their business, and accumulate rental income tax efficiently.

This chapter examines the two most sophisticated SMSF property investment strategies: Australian business real property (BRP) for business owners, and US residential property investment via Delaware LLC for geographic diversification. These strategies operate under completely separate legal and tax frameworks but share one common characteristic: when structured correctly, both can avoid in-house asset classification and deliver exceptional tax outcomes.

Australian business real property leverages Section 66 of the SIS Act (which permits related-party acquisitions of BRP) combined with Division 152 small business CGT concessions (including the 15-year exemption) to transfer commercial premises into an SMSF at minimal tax cost. The business continues to pay rent, but instead of enriching a third-party landlord, the rent builds retirement wealth at 0-15% tax rates.

US residential property leverages a Delaware Limited Liability Company (LLC) that elects corporate tax treatment via IRS Form 8832, qualifying it as a Regulation 13.22C non-geared entity under Australian superannuation law. When all nine Reg 13.22C conditions are met, the SMSF's investment in the LLC is NOT an in-house asset, despite the LLC holding residential (not commercial) property.

Critical Clarification: LLCs Are Companies, Not Trusts

A Delaware LLC is a Limited Liability Company under US state law, it is a company, not a trust. By default, a single-member LLC is treated as a 'disregarded entity' for US federal tax purposes (meaning it's ignored and the owner reports income directly). However, by filing IRS Form 8832, the LLC can elect to be treated as a corporation for tax purposes. Once it elects corporate treatment, the ATO treats the LLC as a company that can qualify under Regulation 13.22C of the SIS Regulations, avoiding in-house asset classification. This Form 8832 election is mandatory for SMSF compliance.

1. AUSTRALIAN BUSINESS REAL PROPERTY: COMPLETE STRUCTURAL FRAMEWORK

1.1 The Business Real Property Strategy Explained

Australian business real property (BRP) is defined under Section 66(5) of the SIS Act as real property used wholly and exclusively in one or more businesses. This definition creates a critical exception to the general prohibition on SMSFs acquiring assets from related parties, enabling business owners to:

- Transfer their business premises from personal ownership into their SMSF
- Have the SMSF purchase premises from a related entity (such as the member's trading company)
- Lease the property back to the operating business at arm's-length market rent
- Build substantial retirement wealth as rent is taxed at 0-15% in the SMSF instead of up to 47% personally

Why This Strategy Is Exclusively Australian:

The Australian small business CGT concessions (Division 152) particularly the 15-year exemption only apply to Australian resident taxpayers disposing of active business assets. US business property does not qualify. Additionally, state stamp duty concessions for BRP transfers are only available in Australian jurisdictions. Therefore, the BRP strategy is designed exclusively for Australian trading businesses with Australian commercial premises.

1.2 Structure Diagram: Direct SMSF Ownership of Business Premises

DIAGRAM 1: Australian BRP – Direct SMSF Ownership

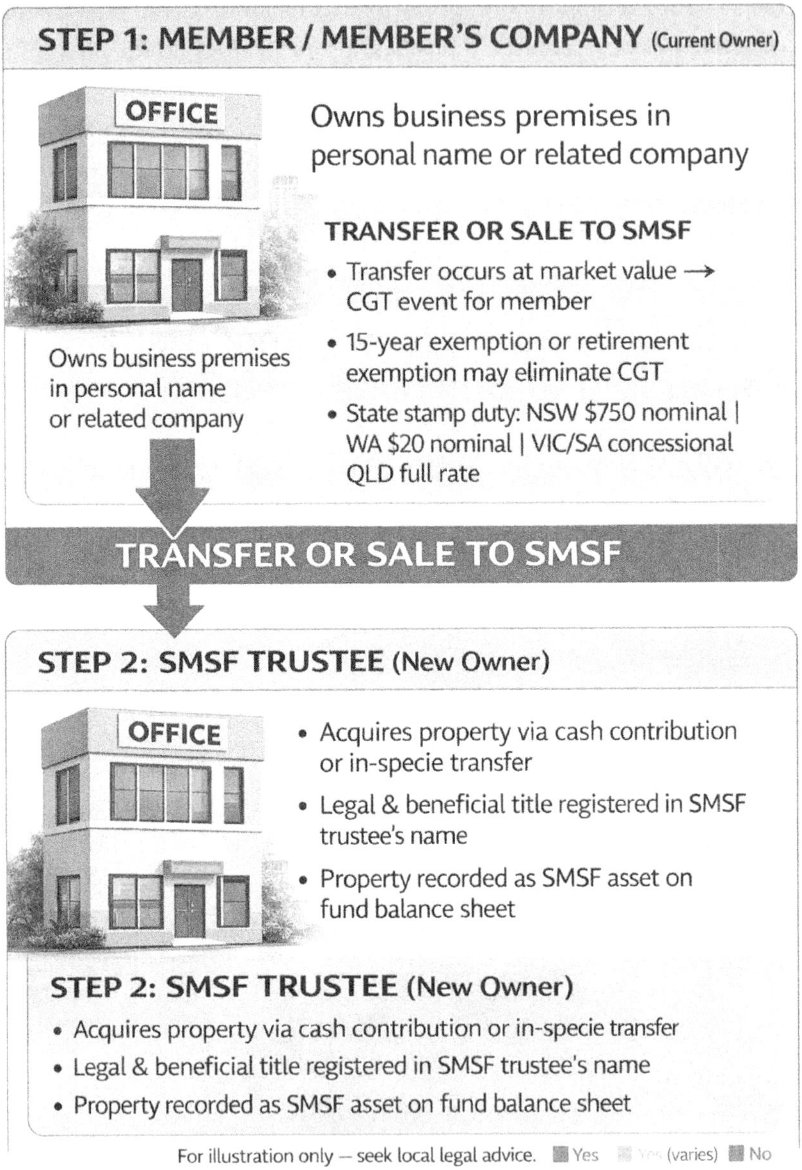
STEP 1: MEMBER / MEMBER'S COMPANY (Current Owner)
OFFICE
Owns business premises in personal name or related company
TRANSFER OR SALE TO SMSF
• Transfer occurs at market value → CGT event for member
• 15-year exemption or retirement exemption may eliminate CGT
• State stamp duty: NSW $750 nominal | WA $20 nominal | VIC/SA concessional QLD full rate
Owns business premises in personal name or related company
TRANSFER OR SALE TO SMSF
STEP 2: SMSF TRUSTEE (New Owner)
OFFICE
• Acquires property via cash contribution or in-specie transfer
• Legal & beneficial title registered in SMSF trustee's name
• Property recorded as SMSF asset on fund balance sheet
STEP 2: SMSF TRUSTEE (New Owner)
• Acquires property via cash contribution or in-specie transfer
• Legal & beneficial title registered in SMSF trustee's name
• Property recorded as SMSF asset on fund balance sheet
For illustration only – seek local legal advice.
Yes
(varies)
No

1.3 Alternative Structure: LRBA Bare Trust

If the SMSF lacks sufficient cash to purchase the business premises outright, it may borrow using a Limited Recourse Borrowing Arrangement (LRBA) under Section 67A of the SIS Act. Legal title is held by a bare trustee until the loan is fully repaid.

DIAGRAM 2: Australian BRP – LRBA Bare Trust Structure

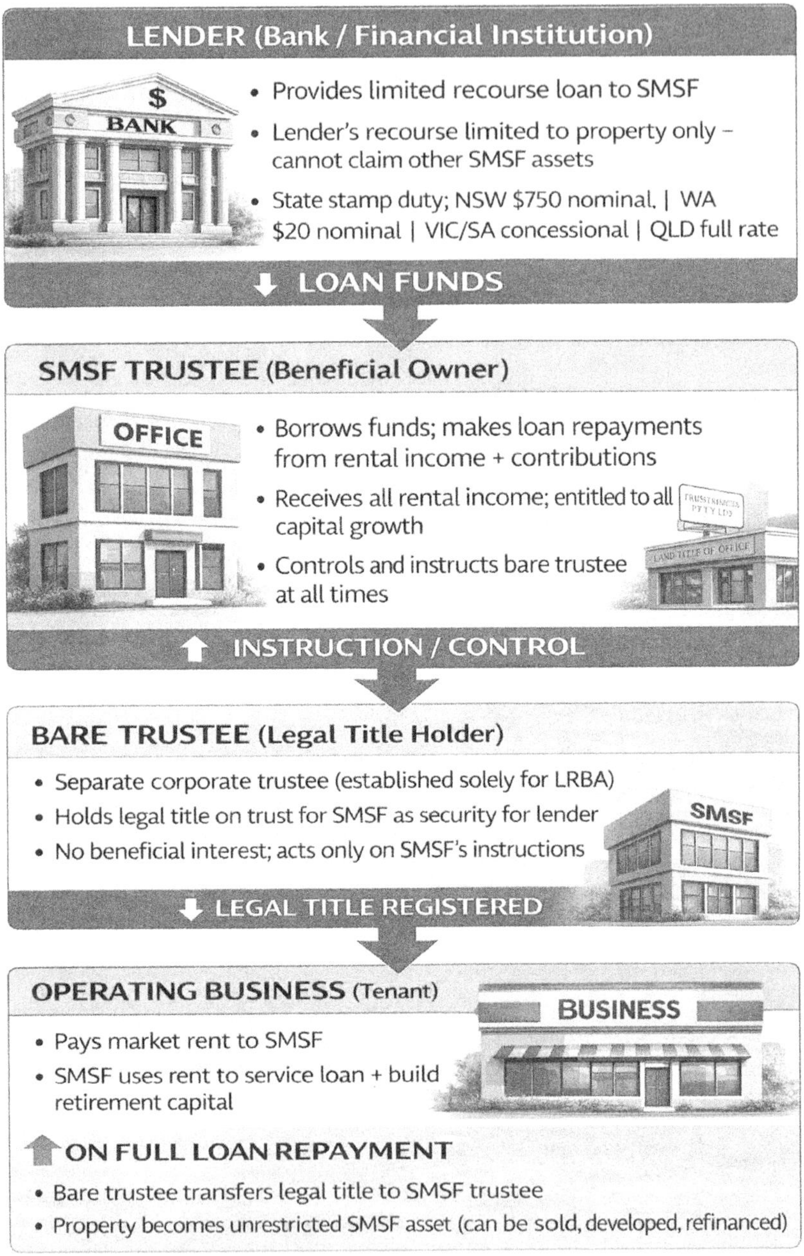

For illustration only – seek local legal advice. Yes (varies) No

1.4 Transferring Existing Business Premises: Tax and Duty Consequences

Most business owners already own their commercial premises. Transferring to the SMSF triggers two tax events:

Federal Capital Gains Tax

The ATO treats the transfer as a disposal at market value, creating an immediate CGT liability. However, Division 152 small business CGT concessions can eliminate this entirely:

Concession	Eligibility Requirements	Effect
15-Year Exemption (Subdiv 152-B)	Property held ≥15 years continuously; owner aged 55+ and retiring OR permanently incapacitated	Entire capital gain disregarded – ZERO CGT
Retirement Exemption (Subdiv 152-D)	$500,000 lifetime cap per individual; if under 55, must contribute exempt amount to super	Up to $500,000 of capital gain exempt over lifetime
50% Active Asset Reduction (Subdiv 152-C)	Property used in active business; basic conditions met (turnover or net asset tests)	50% reduction applied AFTER CGT discount (combined: up to 75% total reduction)

Worked Example: 15-Year Exemption

Sarah, aged 61, has operated her dental practice from a medical suite purchased in 2008 for $380,000. In 2025, the suite is valued at $1.25 million. Sarah is retiring and transferring the suite to her SMSF.

- Capital gain: $1,250,000 − $380,000 = $870,000
- Sarah has held the property for 17 years (✓ ≥15 years requirement met)
- Sarah is 61 and retiring (✓ ≥55 and retiring requirement met)
- Result: Entire $870,000 capital gain is exempt under 15-year exemption
- CGT payable: $0

State Stamp Duty Concessions

State	Concession Type	Conditions	Typical Duty
NSW	Nominal (LRBA)	BRP held in bare trust for SMSF	$750 (fixed)
WA	Nominal	BRP transfer; ongoing sole-benefit test (see warning below)	$20 (nominal)
VIC	Concessional	Related party BRP transfer; various conditions	Varies by value
QLD	Limited/none	No broad BRP concession	Full rate (up to 5.75%)

> **WA Ongoing Compliance Trap**
>
> In WA, the $20 nominal duty is conditional on the property continuing to be held for the sole benefit of transferring members. If the SMSF later admits a second member, or the property benefits other members, the WA Commissioner of State Revenue can retrospectively assess full ad valorem duty on the original transfer. This can result in a six-figure duty bill years after the transfer. Always obtain WA-specific legal advice before proceeding.

Combined Outcome: In NSW or WA, transferring a $1.25 million business premises can cost as little as $20-$750 in total upfront tax (assuming 15-year exemption applies), transforming a substantial business asset into a retirement wealth generator with virtually no tax friction.

2. US RESIDENTIAL PROPERTY: DELAWARE LLC WITH FORM 8832 ELECTION

2.1 Why 95% of International Property Is US Residential

US residential real estate dominates SMSF international property investment for practical reasons:

- Liquidity: Deepest residential property markets globally; transactions settle in 30-60 days
- Transparency: Established title systems, independent valuations, reliable rental data

- Yield: Many US cities offer gross rental yields of 5-8% (vs Australian capital cities 2-4%)
- Diversification: Geographic and currency diversification away from Australian market
- Accessibility: Entry-level condos available from $150-300k USD (~AUD $225-450k)

2.2 Understanding the LLC: US Law vs Australian Tax Treatment

A Delaware Limited Liability Company (LLC) is a legal entity created under Delaware state law. It is a company, not a trust. The LLC provides limited liability protection to its members (owners) similar to a corporation, but with flexible governance and tax treatment options.

US Federal Tax Treatment: The Critical IRS Form 8832 Election

Under IRS regulations, a single-member LLC has two possible tax classifications:

Tax Classification	How Achieved	Tax Consequences
Disregarded Entity (DEFAULT	Automatic if no election filed	LLC ignored for US tax; income flows directly to owner's return
Corporation (ELECTED)	File IRS Form 8832 'Entity Classification Election'	LLC files separate corporate tax return (Form 1120); taxed as corporation

Why Form 8832 Is Mandatory for SMSF Investments

If the LLC remains a disregarded entity (the default), the ATO treats the SMSF as owning the US property directly, not through a separate legal entity. This creates an in-house asset problem because the property is not held through a qualifying Regulation 13.22C company. By filing Form 8832 and electing corporate treatment, the LLC becomes a 'company' for both US and Australian tax purposes, allowing it to qualify under Regulation 13.22C and avoid in-house asset classification. Form 8832 must be filed within 75 days of LLC formation to be effective from inception.

2.3 Australian Treatment: Regulation 13.22C Non-Geared Entity

Regulation 13.22C of the Superannuation Industry (Supervision) Regulations 1994 provides an exemption from in-house asset classification for SMSF investments in related companies or unit trusts, provided the company/trust meets strict conditions at all times.

The Nine Critical Regulation 13.22C Conditions

For the LLC to qualify as a Regulation 13.22C non-geared entity (and thus NOT be an in-house asset), it must meet ALL of the following conditions continuously:

#	Regulation 13.22C Condition	Application to US LLC Holding Residential Property
1	No borrowing: The company cannot have any outstanding borrowings	LLC cannot borrow to purchase or renovate property; SMSF must fund 100% with cash contributions
2	No interest in other entities: Cannot hold shares in companies or units in trusts	LLC holds only the US property (real estate) and cash in its US bank account; no other investments
3	No lending: Cannot lend money to any other person or entity	LLC cannot provide vendor finance or lend to any party (related or unrelated)
4	No charges: Cannot have assets subject to a charge, mortgage, or lien	Property must be unencumbered; no mortgage against the property
5	No leases to related parties (EXCEPT business real property): Cannot lease assets to related parties unless property is BRP	US residential property leased to UNRELATED tenants only (never to SMSF members/family) ✓ Compliant
6	No related-party acquisitions: Cannot acquire assets from related parties after 11 August 1999	Property must be purchased from unrelated third-party seller on open market

7	SMSF must have fewer than 5 members: Standard SMSF membership restriction	SMSF must have 4 or fewer members at all times (most SMSFs comply)
8	Arm's length transactions: All dealings must be on commercial arm's length terms	Property purchased at market price; rent set at market rates; all transactions commercial
9	Cannot conduct a business: The company cannot operate as a trading or development business	LLC holds property for passive investment only (rental income); no development, flipping, or trading

Key Point: Residential Property IS Permitted Under Reg 13.22C

Regulation 13.22C does NOT require the LLC to hold only 'business real property' (commercial property). The business real property restriction (Condition 5) ONLY applies to leases to RELATED parties. Since US residential property is leased to UNRELATED tenants (never to SMSF members or their families), this restriction does not apply. As long as all nine conditions are met, residential property held in a properly structured LLC qualifies under Reg 13.22C and is NOT an in-house asset. This is confirmed by SMSF practitioners and the ATO's interpretation of Regulation 13.22C.

2.4 The Authorised Deposit-Taking Institution (ADI) Requirement

One additional critical compliance requirement: the LLC's US bank account must be held with an Authorised Deposit-Taking Institution (ADI) as defined by APRA.

An ADI is a financial institution authorised to take deposits from the public. In practice, this means major international banks:

- JPMorgan Chase
- Bank of America
- Citibank
- HSBC
- Wells Fargo

If the LLC's bank account is held with a non-ADI bank, the SMSF's investment in the LLC may be treated as an in-house asset because the LLC is effectively providing financial accommodation to a non-approved institution.

2.5 Complete Structure Diagram: US Residential via Delaware LLC

DIAGRAM 3: US Residential Investment – Delaware LLC with Form 8832 Election

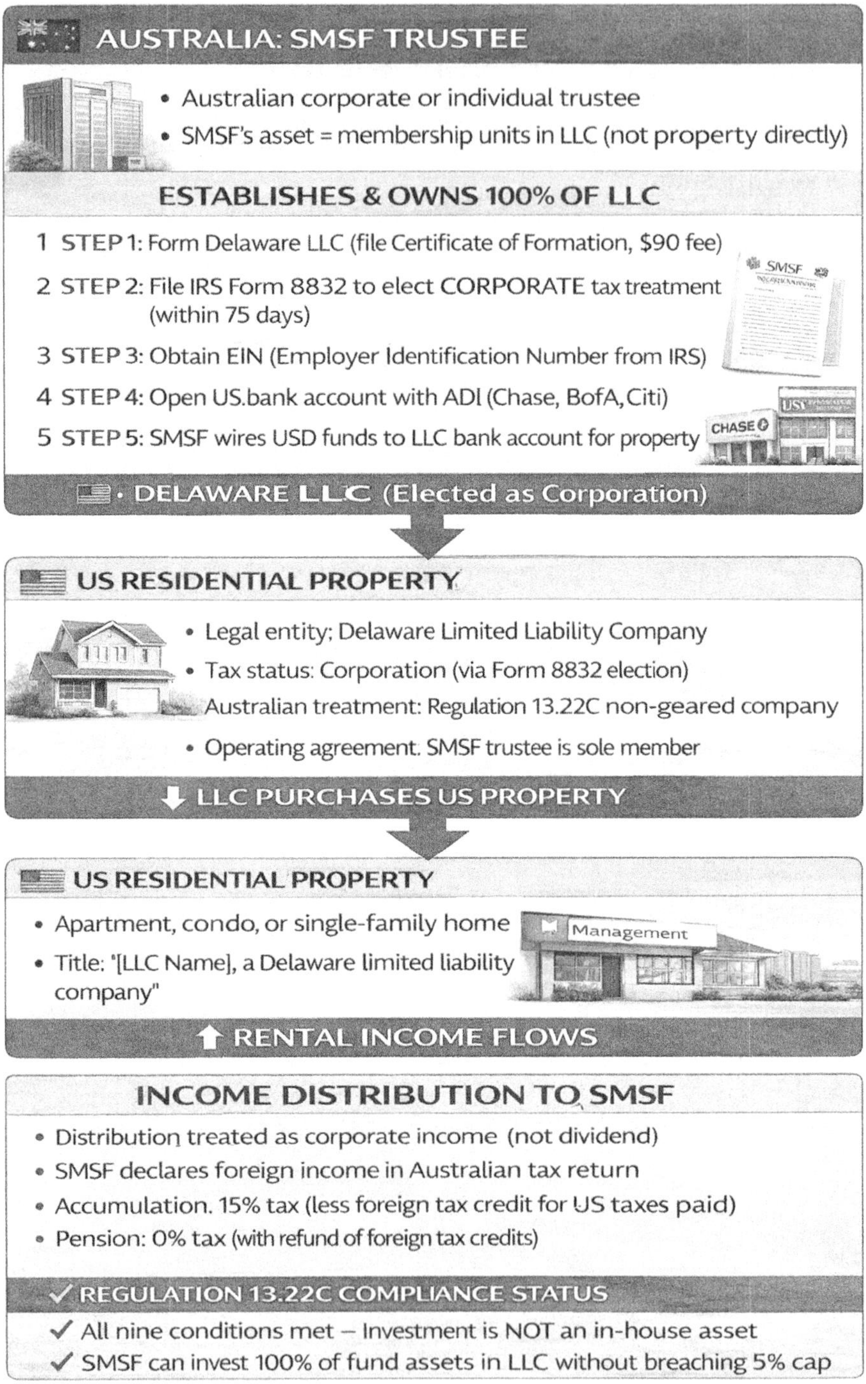
AUSTRALIA: SMSF TRUSTEE
• Australian corporate or individual trustee
• SMSF's asset = membership units in LLC (not property directly)
ESTABLISHES & OWNS 100% OF LLC
1 STEP 1: Form Delaware LLC (file Certificate of Formation, $90 fee)
2 STEP 2: File IRS Form 8832 to elect CORPORATE tax treatment (within 75 days)
3 STEP 3: Obtain EIN (Employer Identification Number from IRS)
4 STEP 4: Open US.bank account with ADI (Chase, BofA, Citi)
5 STEP 5: SMSF wires USD funds to LLC bank account for property
SMSF
CHASE
• DELAWARE LLC (Elected as Corporation)
US RESIDENTIAL PROPERTY
• Legal entity; Delaware Limited Liability Company
• Tax status: Corporation (via Form 8832 election)
Australian treatment: Regulation 13.22C non-geared company
• Operating agreement. SMSF trustee is sole member
LLC PURCHASES US PROPERTY
US RESIDENTIAL PROPERTY
• Apartment, condo, or single-family home
• Title: "[LLC Name], a Delaware limited liability company"
Management
RENTAL INCOME FLOWS
INCOME DISTRIBUTION TO SMSF
• Distribution treated as corporate income (not dividend)
• SMSF declares foreign income in Australian tax return
• Accumulation. 15% tax (less foreign tax credit for US taxes paid)
• Pension: 0% tax (with refund of foreign tax credits)
✓ REGULATION 13.22C COMPLIANCE STATUS
✓ All nine conditions met – Investment is NOT an in-house asset
✓ SMSF can invest 100% of fund assets in LLC without breaching 5% cap

2.6 Step-by-Step Implementation Process

Phase 1: Establish the Delaware LLC and Elect Corporate Treatment

1. Engage US Attorney: Retain US attorney licensed in Delaware to prepare LLC formation documents and operating agreement.
2. File Certificate of Formation: Submit to Delaware Division of Corporations ($90 filing fee + $300 annual franchise tax).
3. Prepare Operating Agreement: Must specify SMSF trustee as sole member with 100% ownership.
4. Appoint Registered Agent: Delaware requires registered agent with physical Delaware address (commercial service, ~$100-300/year).
5. File IRS Form 8832: Critical step – elect corporate tax treatment within 75 days of formation. Without this election, the LLC remains a disregarded entity and cannot qualify under Reg 13.22C.
6. Apply for EIN: File IRS Form SS-4 to obtain LLC's Employer Identification Number (required for banking and tax filings).

Phase 2: Banking and Property Acquisition

7. Open US Bank Account: LLC opens account with ADI (Chase, Bank of America, Citibank, HSBC). Requires EIN, operating agreement, certificate of formation.
8. SMSF Wires Funds: SMSF sends USD funds via international wire to LLC bank account for property purchase.
9. Engage US Real Estate Agent: Licensed agent identifies properties, prepares offers, manages transaction.
10. Property Purchase: LLC purchases property at market value from unrelated seller. Title registered in LLC's name.

Phase 3: Ongoing Operations

11. Engage Property Manager: Local property management company (8-10% of rent) handles tenants, maintenance, rent collection.
12. Income Distribution: Net rental income distributed quarterly from LLC to SMSF via international wire.
13. US Tax Filings: LLC files annual US corporate tax return (Form 1120) reporting rental income and expenses.
14. Australian Tax Reporting: SMSF declares foreign income in annual return, claims foreign tax credits for US taxes paid.

3. STRATEGIC COMPARISON AND COMPLIANCE FRAMEWORK

3.1 Side-by-Side Comparison

Factor	Australian BRP	US Residential (LLC + Form 8832)
Primary Purpose	Business/retirement integration; tax-efficient rent	Investment diversification; geographic/currency hedge
Asset Type	Commercial premises (warehouse, office, medical, retail)	Residential (apartment, condo, single-family home)
Legal Structure	Direct SMSF ownership OR LRBA bare trust	US LLC (must elect corporate treatment via Form 8832)

In-House Asset Status	NOT in-house (Section 66 BRP exemption)	NOT in-house IF all Reg 13.22C conditions met
Related Party Acquisition	PERMITTED (BRP exception)	PROHIBITED (must buy from unrelated seller)
CGT Concessions	15-year exemption; retirement exemption; 50% active asset reduction	None (US has no equivalent for foreign buyers)
Stamp Duty	Nominal in NSW/WA ($20-750); concessional in VIC/SA	Full US transfer tax (varies by state; 1-4% of purchase price)
Tenant	Related party (member's business) PERMITTED	Unrelated party ONLY (never SMSF members/family)
Tax on Rent	Accumulation: 15% | Pension: 0%	US: ~20-30% | Australia: 15% (accum) or 0% (pension) with credit
Minimum Capital	$300k-1m+ AUD (regional commercial premises)	$150-300k USD (~$225-450k AUD entry-level condo)

3.2 Compliance Checklist

Australian BRP Compliance

- ✓ Property used wholly and exclusively for business (no mixed personal use)
- ✓ Formal commercial lease agreement at market rent (independent valuation every 3 years)

- ✓ All trustee decisions documented in minutes with retirement benefit rationale
- ✓ Investment strategy updated to authorise BRP acquisition
- ✓ If transferring existing premises: verify 15-year exemption or obtain CGT tax opinion
- ✓ If transferring: obtain state-specific stamp duty advice before proceeding

US LLC Compliance

- ✓ LLC files IRS Form 8832 to elect corporate treatment within 75 days of formation
- ✓ Operating agreement specifies SMSF trustee as sole member
- ✓ US bank account held with ADI (Chase, BofA, Citi, HSBC, Wells Fargo)
- ✓ All nine Regulation 13.22C conditions met at all times:
  - • No borrowing by LLC
  - • No investments in other entities
  - • No lending
  - • No charges/mortgages on property
  - • Lease to unrelated tenants only
  - • Property acquired from unrelated seller
  - • SMSF has <5 members
  - • All transactions arm's length
  - • No business operations (investment only)
- ✓ Property manager engaged (never self-managed from Australia)
- ✓ LLC files annual US corporate tax return (Form 1120)

- ✓ SMSF declares foreign income; claims foreign tax credits

CONCLUSION: PRECISION IN STRUCTURE, POWER IN EXECUTION

Australian business premises and US residential property represent the two most sophisticated SMSF property strategies available. Both can avoid in-house asset classification when structured correctly, but they achieve this through entirely different legal and regulatory pathways.

Australian BRP: Section 66 of the SIS Act creates a carve-out for business real property, permitting related-party acquisitions that would otherwise be prohibited. Combined with Division 152 small business CGT concessions (particularly the 15-year exemption) and state stamp duty concessions (as low as $20 in WA), business owners can transfer multi-million-dollar premises into their SMSF with minimal upfront tax cost. The business continues to pay rent, but that rent builds retirement wealth at 0-15% tax rates instead of enriching third-party landlords at 47% personal marginal rates.

US Residential via LLC: A Delaware LLC is a company (not a trust) that must elect corporate tax treatment via IRS Form 8832. This election transforms the LLC from a 'disregarded entity' (which would create in-house asset problems) into a corporation that can qualify under Regulation 13.22C of the SIS Regulations. When all nine Reg 13.22C conditions are met – including no borrowing, no related-party leases, and holding only residential property and cash – the SMSF's investment in the LLC is NOT an in-house asset, despite the LLC holding residential (not commercial) property. This allows SMSFs to invest up to 100% of fund assets in US residential real estate without breaching the 5% in-house asset cap.

Critical Success Factors:

- Australian BRP: Verify 15-year exemption applies before transfer; obtain independent valuations; document all decisions in trustee minutes
- US LLC: File Form 8832 within 75 days; use ADI bank; maintain all nine Reg 13.22C conditions continuously
- Both strategies: Engage specialist advisers from day one; update investment strategy; maintain arm's length compliance

The regulatory frameworks governing these strategies have been tested over decades and refined through ATO guidance, court decisions, and practitioner experience. The structures work. The tax outcomes are exceptional. The difference between success and catastrophic failure is precision in implementation. This chapter provides the complete roadmap.

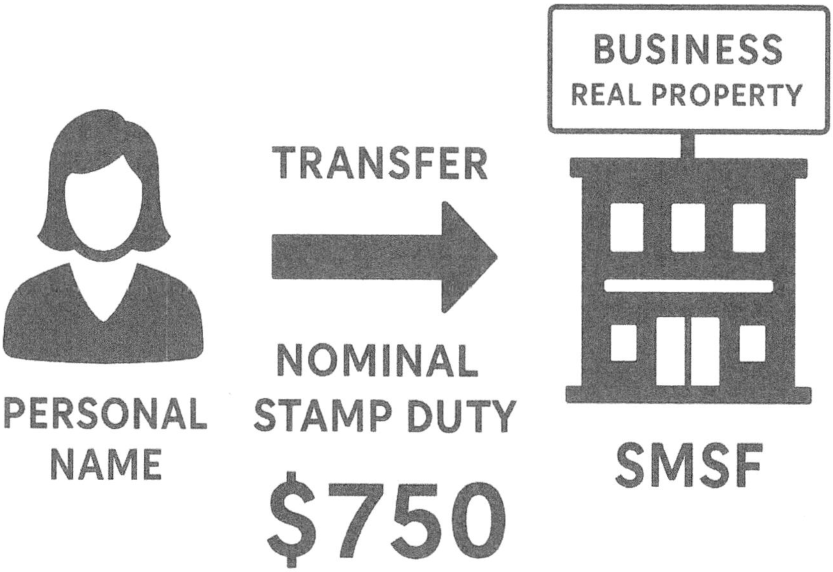

Example NSW

Case Example – (My Business Neighbours' Story)

In my first premises in NSW, my neighbour owned her business unit in her personal name and ran her business from it for over 15 years. As this was a genuine "business real property" and she was effectively just moving it into her SMSF to hold for her retirement benefit, the transfer qualified for nominal duty instead of full stamp duty (in that case, it was only a few hundred dollars at the time, rather than tens of thousands).

However, for tax purposes, the ATO treats the transfer as a sale at market value, which would normally trigger Capital Gains Tax. She was able to rely on the small business CGT concessions, including the 15-year exemption/retirement exemption framework, to reduce or eliminate the gain. Practically, that meant she could move the business unit into her SMSF at minimal upfront tax cost, and from that point forward, her business paid rent to her SMSF, not to her personally. That rent built her retirement savings in a low-tax environment (15% in accumulation, potentially 0% in pension phase).

In summary, moving commercial premises you already own into your SMSF can be one of the cleanest long-term strategies for professionals and business owners: rent is taxed inside super instead of in your personal name, and you effectively warehouse a key business asset for retirement. However, the move is not tax free by default; you rely on (1) state-based nominal duty rules for business real property, and (2) federal small business CGT concessions like the 15-year exemption and the $500,000 retirement exemption. If you don't qualify for those concessions, you can still face a real CGT bill on day one.

Permissible vs. Restricted Countries

SMSF FOREIGN PROPERTY

Country	SMSF Ownership Feasible?	Notes
United States	Yes	High rental yields in some states: SMSF can hold US property direct often via US trust).
United Kingdom	Yes	Established property market: SMSFs can hold UK real estate (via trustee or UK SPV)
New Zealand	Yes	Closely aligned to Australian rules: SMSFs can buy directly as non-residents (subject to NZ Overseas Investment Act rules)
Thailand	No	Foreigners can't hold land; condos (imits to 49% foreign; SMSF ownership effective prohibited
India	No	FDi restrictions on residential/commercial property make direct SMSF investment impra-
Many Euro cou.	Yes	Often allowed but must use a local entity: consult local law

For illustration only – seek local legal advice. Yes Yes (varies) No

As one SMSF specialist notes, "the same stringent regulations that apply to owning Australian property in an SMSF also apply to overseas properties". Always check the trust deed and ensure cross-border taxes and foreign law are navigated properly.

Conclusion

Property investment via an SMSF can be powerful but complex. Owning your business premises within your SMSF creates a tax-efficient integration of business and retirement strategy. Rent becomes an asset, not an expense. Residential property (apartments or houses) can deliver solid long-term growth and income for SMSF members who are comfortable with property management and leverage. International real estate offers diversification but requires careful legal structuring and knowledge of foreign ownership rules.

Each approach has strict compliance requirements: arm's length dealings, sole-purpose test, and investment strategy alignment. The rewards (control, tax efficiency, retirement income) are significant, but so are the potential pitfalls (liquidity constraints, stamp duty and foreign tax rules, strict ATO compliance).

In summary, using an SMSF for property, whether business premises, investment homes, or overseas assets, demands thorough planning and professional guidance. Done correctly, however, it can significantly boost retirement outcomes for small business owners and SMSF trustees.

CHAPTER 6:
SMSF Subdivision Strategies – Unlocking Property Potential

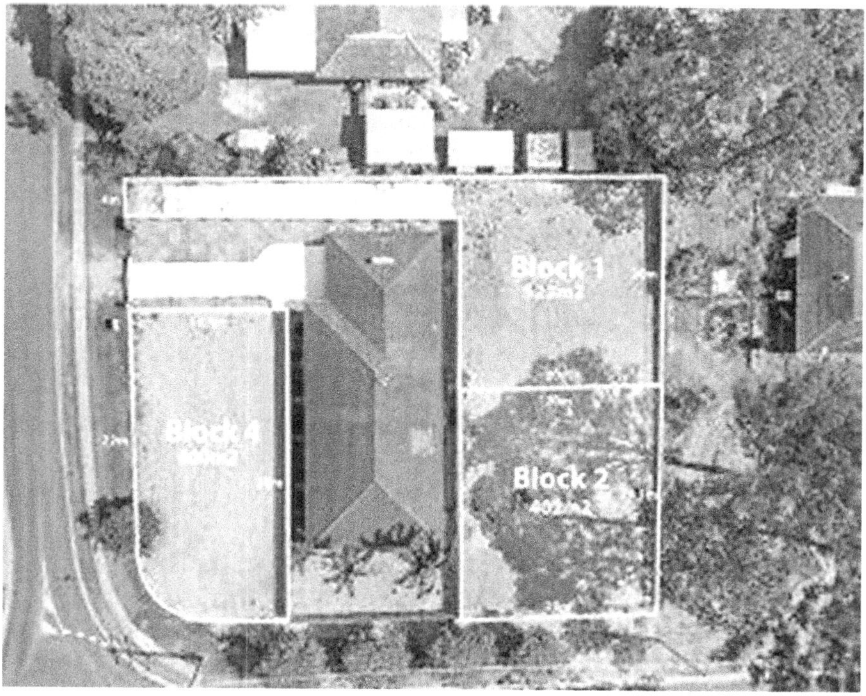

Subdivision projects within an SMSF (*Self-Managed Superannuation Fund*) can transform a single property into multiple income-producing assets. This strategy offers significant potential for capital growth and diversification, but it requires careful planning and strict adherence to regulatory requirements. In this chapter, I explore why SMSFs consider subdivision, the critical legal and tax framework, the step-by-step process for implementation, and advanced strategies to maximise benefits. I, also examine a detailed case study, discuss risk management, and provide a decision-making framework to guide trustees through subdivision projects.

Why Consider Subdivision in an SMSF?
Subdivision within an SMSF can deliver several strategic advantages. By converting one large property into multiple titles, the fund may unlock higher overall value, benefit from diversified income streams, and improve liquidity management.
Capital Growth Potential: Creating multiple titles from one property often increases total value. Smaller subdivided lots can attract a higher price per square meter than a single large block. This premium per square meter can translate into significant capital appreciation. Additionally, having multiple lots provides flexible development or sale options in the future, allowing the SMSF to adapt its strategy as market conditions change.
Enhanced Diversification: Subdividing spreads investment risk across several assets rather than relying on a single tenant or property. Each lot can be leased to different types of tenants (e.g., commercial, medical, industrial), providing a mix of rental incomes. Geographic diversification is also possible if the new lots are situated in different areas of development. This variety of tenants and locations can make the SMSF's income streams more resilient to local market shifts.

Improved Liquidity Management: Holding multiple lots gives the SMSF flexibility to sell assets progressively. Trustees can sell one or more subdivided lots while retaining others, generating liquidity for pension payments or reinvestment without disposing of the entire property. Staggered settlement dates on different lot sales can be used to optimise cash flow timing and meet ongoing fund obligations.

STRATEGIC OVERVIEW: CHOOSING YOUR DEVELOPMENT STRUCTURE

Property development inside superannuation is one of the most powerful and most complex – strategies available to SMSF trustees. When executed correctly, it can transform a single land asset into a diversified portfolio of income-producing lots, delivering both capital growth and improved income yields at highly concessional tax rates. When executed poorly, it can trigger regulatory breaches, disqualification of the fund, and significant penalties under the Superannuation Industry (Supervision) Act 1993 (SIS Act).

The foundational decision every trustee must make before a single dollar is spent is structural: how will the development be legally held, funded, and governed? The choice of structure dictates what you can do, when you can do it, and what tax outcomes will follow. There are four principal structures used in practice:

Structure	Primary Use Case	Can Borrow to Develop?	Key Constraint
SMSF Direct	Straightforward subdivision of SMSF-owned land	No (post-LRBA only)	Single acquirable asset rule during borrowing
Reg 13.22C Non-Geared Trust / Bare Trust	Hold assets without triggering in-house asset rules; LRBA bare trust	No gearing permitted inside trust	Strict non-gearing conditions; no related-party leases except BRP
Unit Trust (unrelated / arm's length)	Joint ventures with unrelated parties; pooled capital	Yes (trust can borrow independently)	In-house asset limit (max 5% of SMSF assets if related)
Discretionary Trust	Estate/family planning alongside SMSF	Yes, but SMSF investment strictly limited	SMSF cannot generally invest in related discretionary trust; serious in-house asset breach risk

Each structure is examined in detail below. Trustees should read this chapter in full before engaging any advisers, as the structural choice fundamentally shapes every subsequent decision: financing, titling, taxation, exit strategy, and estate planning.

2. STRUCTURE A: DIRECT SMSF PROPERTY DEVELOPMENT

2.1 How It Works

The simplest structure is for the SMSF itself to own the land outright and undertake the subdivision or development directly. The fund is both the legal and beneficial owner of the property throughout the entire project. All development costs are paid from fund assets. On completion, the subdivided lots remain SMSF assets until sold or leased.

This structure suits trustees who have already repaid any LRBA on the land (or who acquired it without borrowing), and who have – or can accumulate – sufficient liquid reserves to fund development costs from within the fund.

Key Principle

The SMSF must fund all development costs from its own resources. It cannot draw on an existing LRBA to finance development work, nor can it borrow separately for this purpose in a way that fundamentally changes the acquired asset. Section 67A of the SIS Act restricts borrowing to the acquisition of a 'single acquirable asset' – subdivision creates new assets, moving outside the LRBA framework.

2.2 When SMSF Direct Is the Right Choice

- The land is unencumbered (no LRBA, or the LRBA has been fully repaid).
- The SMSF has sufficient liquidity to cover all development costs without borrowing.
- The development is relatively modest in scale (e.g., a 2-into-3 subdivision rather than a 50-lot estate).
- Trustees want the simplest possible compliance, reporting, and audit trail.
- The exit strategy is to retain and lease lots within the SMSF for ongoing rental income.

2.3 LRBA and the Single Acquirable Asset Rule

This is the area where most SMSF trustees and even some advisers make critical errors. Understanding the interaction between LRBAs and development activity is non-negotiable.

Under section 67A of the SIS Act, an SMSF may borrow money to acquire a single acquirable asset (or a collection of identical assets) under a limited recourse borrowing arrangement. The key restrictions are:

- The borrowed funds may only be used to acquire the asset, not to improve or develop it in a way that changes its character.
- Repairs and maintenance that restore the asset to its pre-existing condition are permitted during the LRBA term.
- Improvements that change the character of the asset – including subdivision, which converts one title into several – are not permitted while borrowings remain outstanding.

ATO Guidance

The ATO has confirmed that subdivision changes the character of a property asset. Converting one title into three new titles means the SMSF no longer holds the same 'single acquirable asset' it borrowed to acquire. Subdivision must therefore be deferred until the LRBA is fully repaid and legal title to the land is transferred from the bare trust to the SMSF.

Issue	SMSF Direct (No LRBA)	SMSF Direct (Post-LRBA Repaid)
Legal title	SMSF holds legal title immediately	Must transfer from bare trust trustee to SMSF first (note duty implications)
Subdivision timing	Can commence at any time	Only after full loan repayment and title transfer
Development funding	Funded from SMSF cash reserves or member contributions	Same – cannot re-borrow under LRBA for development
Stamp duty	No duty on subdivision itself; duty only on sale to third parties	Transfer from bare trust to SMSF may attract duty in some states (seek advice)
CGT on subdivision	Cost base apportioned across new lots; CGT event on subsequent sale	Same treatment

2.4 Step-by-Step Process: SMSF Direct Development

Phase 1 – Strategic Planning and Feasibility

Before any application or expenditure is made, trustees must confirm the project is viable and that the SMSF's investment strategy expressly authorises it.

1. Investment Strategy Review: Formally update the SMSF's written investment strategy to authorise property development. Document the rationale: how does subdivision serve members' retirement objectives? Record this in a trustee resolution.
2. Title and Encumbrance Check: Confirm the SMSF holds unencumbered title (or that the LRBA has been repaid and title transferred). Obtain a current title search.
3. Zoning and Planning Assessment: Engage a town planner to confirm zoning permits subdivision. Identify minimum lot sizes, frontage requirements, environmental overlays, and any council pre-lodgement requirements.
4. Feasibility Analysis: Commission an independent feasibility study covering: (a) total project costs (survey, planning, infrastructure, legal); (b) end-value of each subdivided lot; (c) holding costs and cash flow during the project; (d) sensitivity analysis showing break-even at lower sale prices or higher costs.
5. Liquidity Planning: Model the SMSF's cash position throughout the project. Ensure the fund maintains sufficient liquidity to meet pension payments, tax obligations, and operating costs during the development period. A minimum buffer of 12–18 months of operating expenses is strongly recommended.

Phase 2 – Professional Engagement and Approvals

SMSF property development requires a specialist team. The following professionals should be engaged on arm's-length, market-rate terms:

Professional	Role	SMSF-Specific Considerations
SMSF Legal Adviser	SIS Act compliance, trustee obligations, related-party checks	Must confirm sole purpose test, arm's length, no prohibited transactions
Town Planner	Development application, council liaison, planning strategy	Fees must be market rate; cannot use related party unless arm's length
Licensed Surveyor	Subdivision plan, boundary design, lot configuration	Survey plan is a key audit document; retain original
SMSF Accountant / Tax Adviser	CGT, GST, tax classification, financial reporting	Must determine investment vs business classification; GST registration if required
Conveyancer / Solicitor	Sale contracts, lease agreements, new title registration	All contracts must reflect market terms; document arm's length basis
SMSF Auditor	Independent annual audit; compliance verification	Provide complete documentation pack; early engagement recommended

6. Lodge the development application and pay council fees from the SMSF account (retain receipts).
7. Respond to any requests for additional information from council; document all correspondence.
8. On receipt of development approval, review all conditions and incorporate into the project timeline and budget.
9. Arrange for infrastructure works (roads, services, drainage) by engaging unrelated contractors at market rates.

Phase 3 – Construction, Registration, and Compliance

10. Execute contracts with all contractors. Each contract must be on arm's-length, market-rate terms. Obtain at least two competitive quotes for major works.
11. Maintain a comprehensive record of all payments, variations, and approvals. Use a dedicated SMSF bank account for all project transactions.
12. Hold regular trustee meetings during the construction phase. Document decisions, cost monitoring, and any variations to the original plan.
13. On completion, engage a licensed surveyor to prepare the final plan of subdivision for registration with the relevant land titles office.
14. Register the new titles. Each new lot becomes a separate SMSF asset. Update the SMSF asset register and obtain updated valuations for each lot.

Phase 4 – Post-Subdivision Strategy Execution

With new titles registered, the SMSF can pursue any combination of the following strategies:

- Retain and lease: Hold lots as long-term income-producing assets. Leases must be on market terms. Related-party leases are only permitted for business real property (BRP) at arm's-length commercial rent.
- Progressive sales: Sell one or more lots to generate liquidity. Each sale triggers a CGT event; tax treatment depends on fund phase (accumulation or pension) and holding period.
- Hold for further development: Retain lots in anticipation of rezoning, population growth, or future development opportunities.
- Mixed approach: A combination suited to the members' stage of life and the fund's liquidity requirements.

3. STRUCTURE B: THE REGULATION 13.22C NON-GEARED TRUST

3.1 What Is a Regulation 13.22C Trust?

Regulation 13.22C of the Superannuation Industry (Supervision) Regulations 1994 (SIS Regulations) provides a critical carve-out that allows an SMSF to invest in a related unit trust or related company without that investment counting as an 'in-house asset'. This is significant because the SIS Act (section 71) prohibits an SMSF from having more than 5% of its total assets in 'in-house assets' at any time.

Without the Reg 13.22C carve-out, an SMSF's investment in a related unit trust would immediately be classified as an in-house asset, severely restricting the fund's ability to use this structure. Regulation 13.22C allows the SMSF to invest in a related trust provided the trust meets – and continuously maintains – a strict set of conditions.

Important Distinction: Reg 13.22C vs Bare Trust (Holding Trust)

A 'bare trust' used in an LRBA is a different concept from a Reg 13.22C investment trust. The bare trust (often called a 'holding trust') simply holds legal title to the SMSF's property during the LRBA period – the SMSF remains the beneficial owner at all times. A Reg 13.22C trust, by contrast, is a separate legal entity in which the SMSF holds units, and the trust itself holds and manages assets. Both are referred to in practice as '13.22 trusts' but they serve fundamentally different purposes.

3.2 The Reg 13.22C Conditions: What the Trust Must Never Do

A trust will only qualify for the Reg 13.22C exemption if, at all times, it does NOT:

- Borrow money (the 'non-gearing' condition – this is absolute; any borrowing immediately disqualifies the trust and turns the SMSF's investment into an in-house asset)
- Have a charge over its assets (mortgages, fixed charges, and floating charges are all prohibited)
- Invest in another entity that itself fails these conditions
- Lend money or provide financial accommodation to any person
- Acquire assets from a related party of the SMSF, other than business real property (at market value) or listed securities (at market value)
- Allow a related party of the SMSF to use trust assets for the related party's own benefit, other than on arm's-length terms for business real property leases

Critical Warning

Breaching any single Reg 13.22C condition – even momentarily – causes the SMSF's entire investment in the trust to become an in-house asset with immediate effect. If that investment exceeds 5% of the SMSF's total assets, the fund is immediately in breach of section 83 of the SIS Act, which can result in a contravention notice, administrative penalties, and in serious cases, the fund being made non-complying. Trustees must monitor compliance continuously, not just at year end.

3.3 The Reg 13.22C Trust in Property Development

Within these constraints, a Reg 13.22C non-geared unit trust can be a highly effective vehicle for SMSF property development, particularly when:

- Multiple SMSFs (e.g., one for each family member) wish to pool capital to fund a larger development project.
- The SMSF wants a separate legal entity to hold the development property, providing an additional layer of structural separation.
- Future transfer of units between related parties (e.g., between two SMSFs) is contemplated as part of an estate plan.
- The development involves business real property, which can be leased to related parties (such as a family business) on market terms.

3.3.1 Structure Diagram and Fund Flow

The typical Reg 13.22C structure for development looks like this:

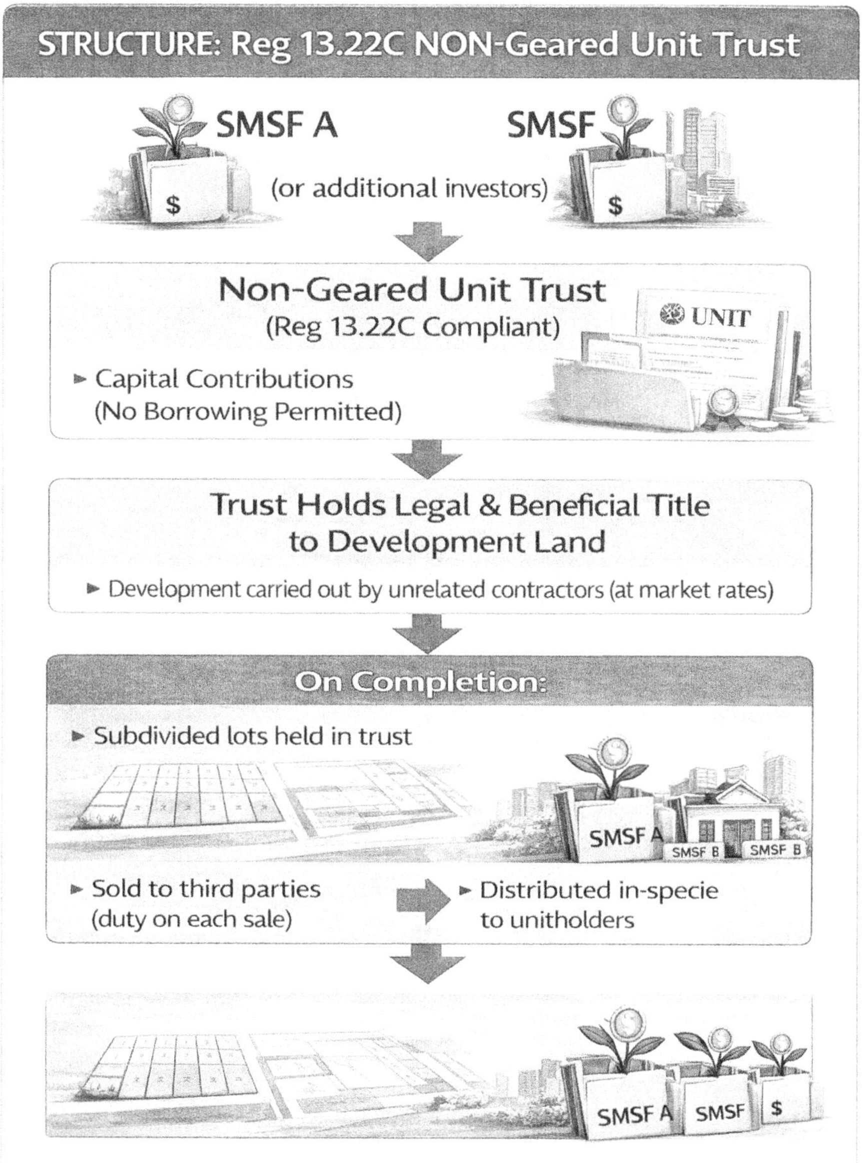
STRUCTURE: Reg 13.22C NON-Geared Unit Trust
SMSF A
SMSF
(or additional investors)
$
$
Non-Geared Unit Trust
(Reg 13.22C Compliant)
UNIT
► Capital Contributions
(No Borrowing Permitted)
Trust Holds Legal & Beneficial Title
to Development Land
► Development carried out by unrelated contractors (at market rates)
On Completion:
► Subdivided lots held in trust
SMSF A
SMSF B
SMSF B
► Sold to third parties
(duty on each sale)
► Distributed in-specie
to unitholders
SMSF A
SMSF
$

3.3.2 Key Advantages of the Reg 13.22C Trust

- Asset pooling: Two or more SMSFs can each hold units in the trust and pool capital to undertake larger projects that would be beyond any single fund.
- Proportional exposure: Each SMSF's economic interest is proportional to its unitholding – no unequal sharing of gains or losses.
- No in-house asset issue: Provided the trust remains compliant, the SMSF's unitholding is not an in-house asset – removing a significant regulatory constraint.
- Structural separation: The trust is a separate legal entity; its assets and liabilities are distinct from the SMSF, providing a degree of ring-fencing.
- Flexibility on exit: Units can potentially be transferred between complying SMSFs, though this requires careful stamp duty and CGT analysis in each state.

3.3.3 Key Limitations and Risks

- No borrowing – ever: The non-gearing condition is absolute. Any finance arrangement within the trust destroys the exemption, potentially creating an immediate SIS Act breach.
- No related-party assets (non-BRP): The trust cannot acquire any asset from a related party of the SMSF unless it is business real property or listed securities at market value.
- Active compliance monitoring: Trustees must monitor the trust's activities at all times, not just at year end. A single inadvertent breach can be catastrophic.
- Cannot lease residential property to related parties: The business real property exemption only applies to genuine

commercial/industrial/agricultural use; residential property leased to a member or relative is never permitted.

- GST and ongoing costs: A separate trust entity requires its own tax file number, ABN, GST registration (if applicable), and annual tax return, adding administrative cost.

3.4 The LRBA Bare Trust (Holding Trust): A Different 13.22 Concept

When an SMSF borrows money under an LRBA, the property being purchased must be held by a separate bare trust trustee – not the SMSF trustee directly – until the loan is repaid. This is sometimes called a 'bare trust' or 'holding trust', and is referenced in regulation 13.22D of the SIS Regulations.

The bare trust arrangement works as follows:

15. The SMSF trustee enters into the LRBA with a lender.
16. The property is purchased in the name of an independent bare trust trustee (often a bare trustee company established for this specific purpose).
17. The bare trust trustee holds legal title on behalf of the SMSF as beneficial owner. The SMSF has all the rights to the income, gains, and eventual legal title.
18. During the loan period, the asset cannot be fundamentally altered. Subdivision is not permitted.
19. When the loan is fully repaid, the bare trust trustee transfers legal title to the SMSF trustee. At this point, subdivision can proceed as a direct SMSF development (see Section 2).

Practical Tip

When establishing a bare trust for an LRBA, use a separate bare trustee company (not an individual trustee of the SMSF) to avoid complications if SMSF trustees change. Ensure the bare trust deed is professionally drafted and specifically identifies the property as held on trust for the SMSF. Retain this documentation permanently as it is fundamental to establishing the SMSF's beneficial ownership for audit and ATO purposes.

4. STRUCTURE C: THE UNIT TRUST (UNRELATED AND RELATED)

4.1 Unit Trusts in the SMSF Context

A unit trust divides the ownership of trust assets into discrete, equal units held by unitholders. An SMSF can invest in a unit trust as a unitholder, with its investment treated as an asset of the fund. The key question for SMSF trustees is whether the unit trust is 'related' to the SMSF or 'unrelated' – this distinction determines whether the investment is subject to the in-house asset rules.

4.2 Unrelated Unit Trusts

If the unit trust is entirely unrelated to the SMSF – meaning no related parties of the SMSF hold any interest in the trust or control its trustee – then the SMSF's investment is simply an asset of the fund. The in-house asset rules do not apply.

This is the most straightforward structure for a genuine joint venture with external, unrelated investors. For example:

- An SMSF contributes $500,000 as a unitholder in a development trust alongside two unrelated developers who each contribute $500,000.
- The trust acquires development land, undertakes the subdivision, and distributes proceeds to unitholders proportionally.
- The trust can borrow money (e.g., a construction finance facility) without triggering any SMSF-specific lending restrictions, because the borrowings are at the trust level, not the SMSF level.

> **Key Advantage**
> An unrelated unit trust can borrow. This is a significant structural benefit compared to the Reg 13.22C non-geared trust, which cannot borrow at all. Where development funding requires leverage, an unrelated unit trust joint venture structure may allow the project to proceed with less capital from the SMSF.

4.3 Related Unit Trusts

A related unit trust is one where related parties of the SMSF hold units or control the trustee. 'Related parties' include members of the SMSF, their relatives (as broadly defined in section 10 of the SIS Act), and entities controlled by members or their relatives.

An SMSF's investment in a related unit trust is an in-house asset unless the trust qualifies as a Reg 13.22C non-geared trust (see Section 3). If the trust does not qualify, the investment is an in-house asset, and the SMSF must ensure its total in-house assets do not exceed 5% of total fund assets.

This creates a practical constraint: a modest SMSF investment in a related development trust may be permissible if it stays within the 5% threshold, but larger investments are typically not viable without Reg 13.22C compliance.

Characteristic	Unrelated Unit Trust	Related Unit Trust
In-house asset?	No	Yes (unless Reg 13.22C compliant)
Can trust borrow?	Yes (commercially)	No (if Reg 13.22C applies) / Limited by 5% cap otherwise
Investment limit	No SMSF-specific limit	5% of total SMSF assets (unless Reg 13.22C)
Related-party leases	Permitted on market terms	Only BRP at arm's length (if Reg 13.22C)
SMSF control of trust	None (or minority)	May be majority; adds compliance complexity
Best suited to	Joint ventures with external developers	Family pooling strategies with multiple SMSFs

4.4 Using a Unit Trust for SMSF Development: Step-by-Step

Step 1: Establish the Trust Deed

Engage a specialist lawyer to draft a unit trust deed. The deed must be tailored to the development purpose, addressing: unit classes, redemption mechanisms, distribution provisions, trustee powers (including development powers), and exit/winding-up provisions. A generic trust deed is insufficient for a property development project.

Step 2: Subscribe for Units

The SMSF subscribes for units in the trust by transferring funds from the SMSF bank account to the trust bank account. This is the SMSF's investment in the trust. The transaction must be documented and conducted at the issue price determined by the trustee.

Step 3: The Trust Acquires the Land

The trust (not the SMSF) acquires the development land. Stamp duty applies on this acquisition in the normal way. If the trust is purchasing from the SMSF, this must be at market value, and careful analysis is required to ensure the transaction does not breach the prohibited transactions provisions of the SIS Act (section 66).

Step 4: Development and Subdivision

The trust undertakes all development activities as the land owner. The trust enters contracts with planners, surveyors, and builders. If the trust is an unrelated trust that can borrow, it may arrange development finance. All costs flow through the trust's accounts.

Step 5: Post-Completion Strategy

Completed lots are held in the trust. The trust then sells lots to third parties (trust receives proceeds, distributes to unitholders proportionally), leases lots (rental income distributed to unitholders), or winds up (assets distributed in specie to unitholders, subject to CGT and duty analysis).

5. STRUCTURE D: THE DISCRETIONARY TRUST – WHY SMSFS MUST USE IT WITH EXTREME CAUTION

5.1 The Fundamental Problem

A discretionary trust (also called a family trust) is one of the most commonly used structures in Australian tax and estate planning. However, for SMSFs, investment in a related discretionary trust is almost always prohibited under the SIS Act's in-house asset rules, and the consequences of getting it wrong are severe.

The core issue is this: an SMSF's investment in, or loan to, a related discretionary trust is an in-house asset (SIS Act, section 71). Unlike the Reg 13.22C carve-out available for unit trusts and companies, there is no equivalent carve-out for discretionary trusts. This means any investment in a related discretionary trust counts toward the 5% in-house asset cap.

Why Is a Discretionary Trust Different From a Unit Trust?

In a unit trust, each unitholder has a fixed, proportional, and quantifiable interest in trust assets. In a discretionary trust, no beneficiary has a 'fixed entitlement' – the trustee has complete discretion over distributions. The SIS Act regulators view this discretionary nature as incompatible with the SMSF's obligation to maintain assets for the sole purpose of providing retirement benefits, because an SMSF holding an interest in a discretionary trust has no certainty about what it will receive from the trust. The ATO has confirmed this view in numerous rulings.

5.2 When Does a Related Discretionary Trust Become an Issue?

A discretionary trust is 'related' to an SMSF if:

- An SMSF member (or their relative) is a trustee of the discretionary trust.
- An SMSF member (or their relative) is a beneficiary of the discretionary trust.
- A related company or entity of the SMSF controls the discretionary trust.

In practice, most family discretionary trusts will be related to the SMSF of family members. An SMSF investing in or lending money to such a trust is immediately creating an in-house asset.

5.3 Permitted SMSF Interactions With Discretionary Trusts

Despite the general prohibition, there are limited circumstances in which an SMSF can legitimately interact with a related discretionary trust:

- Arm's length lease of business real property: The SMSF can own business real property and lease it to a related discretionary trust (or the business it operates) on commercial terms. The lease is not an 'investment in' the trust – it is a lease transaction. This is a common and entirely legitimate structure.
- Arm's length provision of services: The SMSF can contract with the trust for genuine services on arm's-length terms, though this is relatively uncommon in property development contexts.
- Unrelated discretionary trust: If the discretionary trust genuinely has no related parties in common with the SMSF, the investment is not an in-house asset. However, in practice, this is rarely the case in family wealth structuring scenarios.

Practical Guidance

For most families, the right approach is to keep the SMSF and the family discretionary trust as parallel but separate structures. The discretionary trust undertakes commercial or investment activities for the family outside of super. The SMSF manages the retirement pool. The two structures can interact via arm's-length leases (e.g., the SMSF owns a commercial property and leases it to the family business held in the discretionary trust), but the SMSF should not invest in or lend to the discretionary trust.

5.4 Using a Discretionary Trust Alongside (Not Inside) the SMSF

While the SMSF should not invest directly into a related discretionary trust, a sophisticated family wealth structure can use both entities in a complementary way for property development:

- The discretionary trust acquires and develops property outside of the SMSF structure, using its own capital and (if needed) external borrowings.
- The SMSF acquires and holds separate property assets (which may be similar types of property) within the superannuation environment.
- On completion of development, the discretionary trust may sell a completed lot to the SMSF at arm's-length market value – but only if the property is business real property (section 66 of the SIS Act prohibits SMSFs acquiring residential assets from related parties under any circumstances).
- Rental income and capital gains in the SMSF are taxed at concessional superannuation rates; income in the discretionary trust is distributed to beneficiaries at their marginal rates

(potentially including the corporate tax rate of 30% if distributed to a company beneficiary).

This parallel structure provides flexibility for family wealth planning while maintaining the integrity of both the SMSF and the discretionary trust.

6. CRITICAL LEGAL FRAMEWORK AND COMPLIANCE REQUIREMENTS

Regardless of the structure chosen, all SMSF property development activities must satisfy the core compliance pillars of the SIS Act. Non-compliance is not a minor administrative issue – it can result in the fund being declared non-complying, which means the loss of all concessional tax treatment and potentially significant penalties for trustees personally.

6.1 The Sole Purpose Test (Section 62, SIS Act)

The sole purpose test is the foundational rule of SMSF compliance. The fund must be maintained solely to provide retirement benefits to members, or in the event of a member's death, to their dependents or legal personal representatives.

In property development, the sole purpose test requires that:

- Every development decision is made with members' retirement outcomes as the primary motivation.
- No trustee, member, or related party obtains any present-day benefit from the development activity (e.g., personal use of the

property during development, discounted rents, or personal employment on the development).

- The development strategy is documented in the SMSF's investment strategy and trustee minutes, explicitly articulating the retirement benefit rationale.
- If the development generates income or gains that are reinvested in the fund, that reinvestment is for retirement purposes.

Red Flag Example

A trustee who directs SMSF development funds to employ their spouse's building company – even at market rates – may face ATO scrutiny over whether the development is being conducted at arm's length and whether there is an indirect current-day benefit to the trustee. All engagements with related parties must be robustly documented and commercially justified.

6.2 Arm's Length Requirement (Section 109, SIS Act)

Every transaction the SMSF enters into must be conducted and maintained on arm's-length terms. For property development, this means:

- All professional engagements (planners, surveyors, builders, lawyers) must be at market rates. Obtain at least two competitive quotes for significant engagements.
- Any lease of a completed lot must be at market rent, supported by an independent rental valuation. This applies to all tenants, including unrelated ones.
- Any sale of a completed lot must be at market value, supported by an independent valuation. This is especially critical for any sale

to a related party (subject to the additional restrictions in section 66).

- If the SMSF uses a related-party service provider (which is rarely advisable), that party must charge no less than they would charge an unrelated client for identical services.

6.3 Prohibited Acquisitions (Section 66, SIS Act)

Section 66 imposes strict restrictions on what an SMSF can acquire from related parties. The key rules are:

- An SMSF cannot acquire an asset from a related party unless the asset is: (a) a listed security acquired at market value, or (b) business real property acquired at market value.
- Business real property is broadly defined as real property used wholly and exclusively in a business carried on by the related party. Vacant land being developed is not BRP until it is actually used in a business.
- Residential property can never be acquired from a related party, regardless of price or circumstances. This rule is absolute.
- The corollary: an SMSF selling a completed residential lot to a member or relative is also problematic; trustees should seek legal advice before structuring any exit involving related parties.

6.4 Stamp Duty: When Does It Apply?

A frequently misunderstood area is when stamp duty (transfer duty) applies in SMSF subdivision. The rules can be summarised as follows:

Subdivision Itself: Generally No Duty

When an SMSF already owns a property and subdivides it, the act of subdivision alone does not trigger transfer duty in most Australian states and territories. This is because subdivision does not change the beneficial ownership of the land – the SMSF still owns it, just now with multiple titles instead of one. Revenue offices assess duty on transfers of dutiable property (changes of ownership), not on the redrawn of boundary lines within the same ownership.

Sale of a New Lot to an External Buyer: Duty Applies to the Buyer

When a subdivided lot is sold to a third party, that purchaser pays normal ad valorem stamp duty based on the purchase price or market value (whichever is higher) under the relevant state's rates. This is a standard property purchase and no SMSF-specific concession applies to the buyer.

In-Specie Distribution of a Lot to a Member: Duty Likely Applies

If the SMSF transfers a completed lot to a member as part of a pension payment or benefit payment (a distribution in specie), revenue offices in most states will assess transfer duty on the market value of the lot, because there has been a change in beneficial ownership. There is generally no SMSF-specific concession for this type of in-specie transfer, particularly for residential or development lots. Trustees should seek state-specific stamp duty advice before structuring any in-specie distribution.

Transfer from Bare Trust to SMSF (Post-LRBA)

When the LRBA is repaid and legal title is transferred from the bare trustee to the SMSF trustee, some states may assess duty on this transfer. However, many states have exemptions or concessions for this specific step, recognising that the SMSF was always the beneficial owner. This is highly state-specific and must be confirmed with a local property lawyer before the LRBA is established.

Transaction	Duty?	Notes
Subdivision of SMSF-owned land (no change in ownership)	Generally No	Confirm with state revenue office; some minor administrative charges may apply
Sale of subdivided lot to external third party	Yes – buyer pays	Normal ad valorem rates apply on purchase price / market value
In-specie distribution of lot to SMSF member	Usually Yes	Assessed on market value; no general SMSF exemption in most states
Transfer from LRBA bare trust to SMSF on loan repayment	State-specific	Many states exempt this; must confirm before LRBA established
SMSF selling BRP lot to related party (business entity)	Yes – buyer pays	At market value; normal duty rates apply

7. TAX IMPLICATIONS AND PLANNING STRATEGIES

7.1 Capital Gains Tax (CGT)

CGT treatment is one of the primary reasons SMSF property development is so compelling as a strategy. The concessional rates available to SMSFs are far lower than personal or corporate rates, and pension-phase exemption can eliminate CGT entirely.

Fund Phase	Asset Held	Gross CGT Rate	Effective Rate	Discount
Accumulation	< 12 months	15%	15%	None
Accumulation	≥ 12 months	15%	10%	1/3 discount
Pension Phase (tax-exempt)	Any period	0%	0%	N/A
Mixed (part accumulation, part pension)	≥ 12 months	Proportional	Varies	Proportional

The practical implication is clear: timing the sale of subdivided lots to coincide with the pension phase of the SMSF – or transitioning members to pension phase before a major lot sale – can eliminate CGT entirely. This is a legitimate and widely-used strategy, provided the transition to pension phase is genuine and not contrived solely for tax avoidance purposes.

Example: An SMSF in accumulation phase sells a lot for a $400,000 capital gain after holding for 18 months. The 1/3 discount reduces the taxable gain to $266,667, and CGT at 15% is $40,000. If instead the trustee had transitioned to pension phase before the sale, the entire $400,000 gain would be tax-free, a saving of $40,000.

7.2 Investment vs Business Classification

One of the most critical tax determinations in SMSF property development is whether the activity constitutes a passive investment (subject to CGT rules) or an active business or enterprise (subject to ordinary income tax rules). The distinction has major implications:

Factor	Investment (CGT Treatment)	Business / Enterprise (Income Treatment)
Nature of activity	Hold property for long-term capital growth; incidental subdivision	Systematic, repetitive development; profit-making scheme
Tax treatment of proceeds	Capital gain – CGT rules apply; 1/3 discount available	Ordinary income – no CGT discount; land treated as trading stock
CGT discount availability	Yes (for assets held ≥ 12 months)	No

Tax rate in accumulation	Effective 10% (with discount)	15% on full income
GST registration	Only if turnover exceeds $75k	Required if enterprise threshold met
GST on sales	Generally input-taxed (no GST)	10% GST on sale of new lots (with input credit entitlement)

Indicators of business/enterprise activity that the ATO will consider include: the number of subdivisions being undertaken, the frequency and scale of development activity, the extent to which development is an organised and systematic undertaking, the SMSF's stated purpose in its investment strategy, and the presence of a profit-making intention. Trustees undertaking larger-scale subdivisions (e.g., more than five to six lots, repeated projects, or significant civil works) should obtain a specific tax opinion from an experienced SMSF tax adviser before commencing.

7.3 GST Considerations

GST obligations in SMSF property development are complex and can significantly affect project economics. Trustees must model GST cash flows as part of the feasibility analysis.

Development Scenario	GST Registration	GST on Sales	Input Tax Credits	Margin Scheme?
Passive investment subdivision (non-new residential, not enterprise)	Only if > $75k taxable supplies	Generally none (input-taxed)	Limited	N/A
Enterprise – new residential lots	Required	10% (or margin scheme)	Yes	Available
Enterprise – new commercial / industrial lots	Required	10%	Yes	Generally not needed
Selling existing (non-new) commercial lots	Required if registered	10% (going concern exemption may apply)	Yes	N/A

The margin scheme is particularly important for residential development. Where GST applies to the sale of new residential premises, the margin scheme can significantly reduce the GST liability by calculating GST only on the 'margin' (sale price less purchase price) rather than on the full sale price. To use the margin scheme, both the SMSF (as seller) and the buyer must agree in writing before settlement.

7.4 Income Tax on Rental Income and Deductions

Rental income from development lots retained by the SMSF is subject to the fund's normal tax rates: 15% in accumulation phase, 0% in pension phase. The SMSF can claim the following deductions against rental income in the accumulation phase:

- Interest on LRBA borrowings attributable to the property (during the LRBA period)
- Property management fees
- Council rates and land taxes (not payable by tenants)
- Insurance premiums
- Maintenance and repairs (to restore existing condition, not capital improvements)
- Depreciation on buildings constructed post-1987 at 2.5% per annum (capital works allowance)
- Depreciation on plant and equipment (fixtures, fittings, air conditioning) under effective life schedules
- Legal costs attributable to the income-producing activity

7.5 PAYG Variations to Fund Development and LRBA Repayments

Trustees who are employed individuals can use the PAYG withholding variation system to improve cash flow for SMSF contributions and loan servicing. This strategy works as follows:

20. The trustee engages a tax agent to calculate the expected tax position for the year, taking into account expected SMSF contributions (as personal deductible contributions, if eligible) and any rental losses or deductions.
21. A PAYG variation is lodged with the ATO, requesting a reduction in the withholding rate applied to the trustee's salary.
22. The ATO approves the variation; the employer withholds less tax from the trustee's pay.
23. The trustee uses the additional net pay to make concessional contributions to the SMSF (up to the $30,000 per annum cap for 2025-26).
24. The SMSF uses the additional contributions to fund development costs or LRBA repayments.

This strategy effectively accelerates the accumulation of SMSF capital and reduces the trustee's personal tax liability by bringing forward deductible contributions, without creating additional complexity at the fund level.

7.6 Superannuation Contribution Caps (2025-26)

Contribution Type	2025-26 Annual Cap	Tax on Entry	Key Strategy
Concessional (employer SG + salary sacrifice + personal deductible)	$30,000	15%	Reduce personal marginal tax; fund development costs
Non-concessional (after-tax)	$120,000	Nil	Inject capital for development; no tax cost on entry
Non-concessional – bring-forward rule (under age 75)	$360,000 over 3 years	Nil	Front-load capital for large projects; maximise fund in first year

8. CASE STUDY: REGIONAL MIXED-USE SUBDIVISION – FOUR STRUCTURAL APPROACHES

8.1 Background Facts

The Johnson Family SMSF owns a 2.5-hectare commercial block on the outskirts of a growing regional city in Queensland, purchased in 2018 for $750,000. By 2024, zoning changes permit mixed-use development. An independent valuation establishes the block is worth $1.2 million as a single parcel. A feasibility study confirms the block can be subdivided into three lots of approximately 0.7–1.0 hectares each. Total development costs (survey, planning, infrastructure) are estimated at $180,000. Market research confirms strong demand for smaller commercial lots. The trustee couple, Robert and Jane Johnson, are 58 and 55 respectively.

ely. The SMSF has total assets of $2.1 million, including the property. The LRBA on the property was fully repaid in 2022 and legal title was transferred to the SMSF.

Structure	Advantages	Disadvantages	Recommended For
SMSF Direct	Simplest compliance; no additional entities; all tax benefits stay in SMSF	No external capital; SMSF must fund all costs from reserves	Sufficient SMSF liquidity; sole SMSF project
Reg 13.22C Unit Trust	Can pool with related SMSF (e.g., sibling's fund); structural separation; no IHA issue	Cannot borrow; ongoing trust compliance; additional entity cost	Multi-SMSF families; larger projects needing pooled capital
Unrelated Unit Trust JV	Can borrow; can bring in third-party investors; no IHA limit	Loss of SMSF control; JV complexity; governance risk	Large developments needing leverage and third-party expertise
Discretionary Trust	Estate planning flexibility outside SMSF; full trustee discretion on distributions	SMSF cannot invest; must be run in parallel, not integrated; no super tax rate	Family wealth planning alongside SMSF, not as replacement

8.2 Structural Analysis: Choosing the Right Approach

The trustees consider four structural approaches, each with different legal, tax, and strategic implications:

The trustees choose the SMSF Direct structure, given that: (a) the LRBA is repaid; (b) the SMSF has $420,000 in cash reserves; (c) the development is modest in scale; and (d) they want to maintain full control and capture all tax benefits within the superannuation environment.

8.3 Implementation

Phase 1 – Strategy and Feasibility: The trustees update the SMSF investment strategy, record a trustee resolution confirming the subdivision aligns with retirement income objectives, and commission an independent feasibility study confirming project viability. The fund maintains $240,000 in cash reserves after earmarking $180,000 for development costs (plus a $60,000 contingency).

Phase 2 – Professional Team: The SMSF engages (all at market rates, documented by quotes): a town planner at $15,000; a licensed surveyor at $12,000; an SMSF lawyer at $8,000; and an SMSF-specialist accountant for tax planning at $6,000. Total professional fees: $41,000. Infrastructure works (roads, services, drainage): $145,000.

Phase 3 – Council Approval and Construction: The development application is lodged. Council approves the plan eight months later, subject to conditions. Infrastructure is constructed over four months. Total development expenditure: $186,000 (slightly over budget due to unforeseen drainage requirements – within the contingency buffer).

Phase 4 – Registration and Strategy: Three new titles are registered. The SMSF updates its asset register and obtains independent valuations for each lot.

8.4 Subdivision Outcomes and Financial Performance

Lot	Size	Strategy	2024 Market Value	Annual Net Rent
Lot 1	1.0 ha	Long-term lease – national logistics tenant; 5-year lease, CPI-linked rent reviews	$580,000	$48,000
Lot 2	0.8 ha	Lease to medical centre (business real property; unrelated tenant)	$450,000	$36,000
Lot 3	0.7 ha	Sold at market value to generate liquidity for member pensions	$420,000 (proceeds)	—
TOTAL	**2.5 ha**	**Diversified: income + capital event**	**$1,450,000**	**$84,000 p.a.**

Financial Summary

- Total SMSF investment (purchase + development): $936,000 ($750,000 + $186,000)
- Combined value of lots retained (Lots 1 + 2): $1,030,000
- Sale proceeds from Lot 3: $420,000
- Total value generated: $1,450,000
- Net gain above total investment: $514,000 (55% gain overall)
- Annual rental income from retained lots: $84,000 (approximately 9% yield on original purchase cost)

CGT on Lot 3 Sale

The SMSF has been in pension phase since Robert turned 60 in 2022 (all assets supporting pension). The gain on Lot 3 is entirely tax-free. The proportioned cost base allocated to Lot 3 is approximately $210,000 (based on relative values). The capital gain of approximately $210,000 ($420,000 less $210,000 cost base) is 0% tax in pension phase – saving approximately $21,000 in CGT that would have been payable in accumulation phase (after discount).

8.5 Lessons from the Case Study

- Timing the pension phase transition before major lot sales eliminates CGT – one of the most powerful and legitimate tax strategies available to SMSF trustees.
- Retaining high-quality commercial tenants in subdivided lots generates stable, tax-advantaged rental income that directly supports pension payments.

- Maintaining a cost contingency buffer (in this case $60,000) prevented the fund from needing emergency contributions to cover the cost overrun.
- Engaging specialist professionals with SMSF experience – not just general property professionals – is essential to ensure the compliance requirements are met at every step.
- Comprehensive documentation (strategy update, feasibility study, trustee minutes, contractor quotes, valuations, audit workpapers) reduced audit risk and provided a complete narrative of the project's compliance with the sole purpose test.

Risk Category	Specific Risk	Likelihood / Impact	Mitigation Strategy
Financial	Cost overruns exceeding contingency; project costs absorb pension liquidity	Medium / High	15-20% contingency; stage development; maintain 12-18 month operating reserve
Regulatory – SIS Act	Inadvertent breach of sole purpose, arm's length, or in-house asset rules	Low / Very High	Engage SMSF-specialist advisers; conduct pre-commencement compliance review; regular audit touchpoints
Regulatory – LRBA	Commencing subdivision before LRBA fully repaid; asset character change	Medium / Very High	Obtain loan payoff confirmation; transfer title before any subdivision activity; document all steps
Tax	Misclassification as business enterprise; incorrect GST treatment; CGT on pension transition timing	Medium / High	Obtain specific tax opinion before project commencement; model multiple tax scenarios; review annually
Market	Demand for completed lots weaker than projected; property market downturn during project	Medium / Medium	Conservative value assumptions; pre-commencement market research; retain flexibility on sale timing

Planning / Approval	Development application refused or subject to onerous conditions; council delays	Low-Medium / High	Pre-lodgement meeting with council; engage experienced town planner; build approval timeline into feasibility
Liquidity	SMSF unable to meet pension payments during development period; forced sale at distressed price	Low / Very High	Detailed cash flow modelling before commencement; hold minimum 12 months pension payments in liquid assets; stage contribution strategy
Trustee / Governance	Related-party contracts; trustee conflict of interest; inadequate documentation	Medium / High	Document all decisions; obtain independent valuation for all transactions; avoid related-party contractors unless genuinely arm's length

9. RISK MANAGEMENT FRAMEWORK

Subdivision and development projects within an SMSF carry a distinct risk profile. The following risk categories and mitigation strategies apply across all structural approaches.

10. TRUSTEE DECISION-MAKING FRAMEWORK

Before committing to an SMSF property development project, trustees should work through the following structured decision framework. Each gate must be passed before proceeding to the next.

Gate 1: Structural Eligibility

- Is the SMSF the outright owner of the property (no LRBA outstanding, or LRBA fully repaid and title transferred)?
- If an LRBA exists, has the fund obtained a firm timeline for repayment that defers all development activity until after repayment?
- Is the proposed development consistent with the sole purpose test? Can the trustee document the retirement benefit rationale clearly?
- Has a related-party analysis been conducted? Are all contractors and counterparties unrelated (or provably arm's length)?

Gate 2: Structural Choice

- Does the fund have sufficient liquidity to fund all development costs without borrowing (SMSF direct or Reg 13.22C trust)? Or is a borrowing-capable structure needed (unrelated unit trust)?
- Are multiple SMSFs or investors involved? If so, is a Reg 13.22C unit trust or unrelated unit trust appropriate?
- Is the intention to involve a family discretionary trust? If so, is the SMSF's role limited to a parallel arm's-length lease arrangement (not an investment in the trust)?

Gate 3: Financial Feasibility

- Does the independent feasibility study confirm positive returns under conservative assumptions (e.g., 10-15% lower sale values, 10-20% higher costs)?
- Does the SMSF maintain sufficient liquidity (minimum 12-18 months operating costs plus pension payments) throughout the development period?
- Has the CGT and GST impact been modelled in detail, including the effect of pension phase timing?
- Are the contribution caps (concessional $30,000, non-concessional $120,000) adequate to fund any capital shortfall, or is a PAYG variation strategy required?

Gate 4: Implementation Readiness

- Is the specialist professional team (SMSF lawyer, town planner, surveyor, SMSF accountant, SMSF auditor) engaged and briefed?
- Has the SMSF investment strategy been updated to authorise the development activity?
- Has a trustee resolution been passed and minuted, documenting the rationale and structure?
- Is a comprehensive documentation protocol in place for the full project lifecycle?

Final Suggestion

Treat every SMSF development project as a compliance exercise first and an investment opportunity second. The tax advantages are real and significant but they are only available to trustees who maintain impeccable compliance with the SIS Act throughout. Invest in specialist advice at the outset. The cost of getting it right at the planning stage is a fraction of the cost of remedying a breach after the fact.

11. COMPLIANCE CHECKLIST AND DOCUMENTATION REQUIREMENTS

Pre-Subdivision / Pre-Development

- Updated SMSF investment strategy authorising development activity
- Trustee resolution approving the project, with documented rationale
- Title search confirming SMSF ownership (and confirming no LRBA charge)
- Independent feasibility study and market analysis
- Related-party register: confirm all professional engagements are arm's length
- Tax opinion on investment vs business classification and GST obligations
- CGT modelling including pension-phase transition analysis
- Contribution and liquidity strategy document

During Development

- Development application documents and council correspondence
- All contractor quotes, contracts, and invoices (minimum two quotes for major engagements)
- Trustee meeting minutes at each major project milestone
- Budget vs actual cost monitoring reports
- Compliance review notes from SMSF adviser at key stages
- Bank account statements showing all project expenditures

Post-Subdivision / Post-Development

- Registered survey plan and new certificate(s) of title
- Independent valuation for each new lot at completion
- Updated SMSF asset register reflecting new lot values
- Lease agreements (market rent supported by independent rental appraisal) or sale contracts
- CGT calculation workpapers including cost base apportionment across lots
- GST reconciliation and BAS lodgements (if applicable)
- Auditor's working papers and compliance checklists for annual SMSF audit

12. CONCLUSION AND STRATEGIC RECOMMENDATIONS

SMSF property development whether conducted directly by the fund or through a carefully selected trust structure represents one of the most powerful strategies available to sophisticated superannuation investors. The combination of concessional tax rates, pension-phase CGT exemption, diversification benefits, and income yield potential can materially enhance members' retirement outcomes when the strategy is executed correctly.

The critical success factors are:

- Structural precision: Choose the right vehicle for your specific circumstances direct SMSF, Reg 13.22C non-geared trust, unrelated unit trust, or a parallel discretionary trust arrangement. The wrong structure can be devastating from a compliance and tax perspective.
- LRBA discipline: Respect the single acquirable asset rule absolutely. Subdivision cannot occur while an LRBA is outstanding. Plan the project timeline around full loan repayment.
- Sole purpose and arm's length: Document every decision. Every transaction must be on market terms. Every professional must be engaged at commercial rates. The retirement benefit rationale must be clearly articulated and maintained throughout.
- Tax planning integration: Model CGT and GST outcomes in detail before commencing. Time major sale events to coincide with pension phase where genuine and possible. Use the contribution caps and PAYG variation strategy to fund development costs tax-effectively.
- Risk management: Maintain adequate liquidity. Budget conservatively. Engage specialist professionals. Monitor compliance continuously.

Trustees who follow these principles will find that SMSF property development is not merely viable it is among the most tax-efficient property investment strategies available anywhere in the Australian financial landscape.

Risk Factors

Risk Factor	Probability	Impact	Risk	Mitigation	Mitigation
Council Approval Delays	Medium	High	High		Expedite planning processes
Cost Overruns	Medium	Medium	High		Establish contingencies
Market Downturn	Low	Medium	High		Diversify investments
Regulatory Changes	Low	Medium	High		Stay Informed and adaptable
Cash Flow Strain	Medium	Medium	High		Maintain a buffer

Subdivision Process for SMSFs

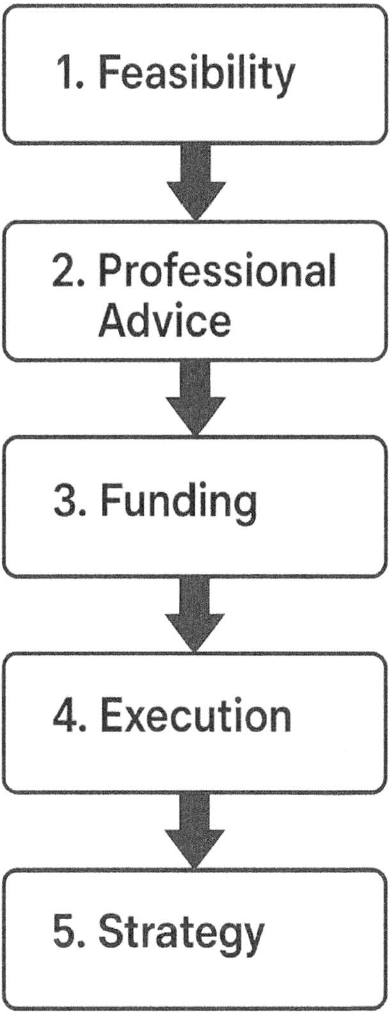

CHAPTER 7:
Tax Efficiencies and Mitigation – Property in an SMSF

Investing in property through an SMSF offers significant tax advantages. Trustees can benefit from concessional tax rates, deductions on property expenses and loan interest, and favourable treatment of capital gains. This chapter focuses on tax strategies for property investments in an SMSF, incorporating the updated 2024-25 superannuation rates and thresholds, including options to use PAYG variations to assist with loan repayments.

1. Tax Rates for SMSF Property Investments (2025-26)

In 2025-26, the tax rates applicable to SMSF property investments remain highly concessional compared to personal investments. Here is how SMSF tax rates apply to property investments:

- **Accumulation Phase:** The SMSF's earnings, including rental income and capital gains, are taxed at 15%. Property held for more than 12 months is eligible for a one-third capital gains tax (CGT) discount, effectively reducing the CGT rate to 10%.
- **Pension Phase:** Once the SMSF enters the pension phase, all earnings, including rental income and capital gains, are tax-free.

These concessional rates provide a major advantage over personal tax rates, which can be as high as 47% (including the Medicare Levy).

2. Capital Gains Tax (CGT) on Property Sales

Capital gains tax is a key consideration when selling property within an SMSF. The way capital gains are taxed depends on whether the SMSF is in the accumulation or pension phase.

a) CGT in the Accumulation Phase

In the accumulation phase, any capital gains realised from the sale of property are taxed at 15%. However, for properties held for more than 12 months, the SMSF qualifies for a one-third CGT discount, which reduces the effective CGT rate to 10%.

- **Example:** If an SMSF sells a property for a $300,000 gain after holding it for more than 12 months, the taxable capital gain is reduced to $200,000 after applying the 2/3 discount, and the CGT payable would be $30,000 (15% of $200,000, which equates to an effective rate of 10% on the original gain).

b) CGT in the Pension Phase

Once the SMSF enters the pension phase, all capital gains are completely tax-free. This offers a significant advantage for trustees who defer the sale of property until they reach retirement.

- **Example:** If an SMSF sells a property for a $500,000 gain during the pension phase, the entire gain is tax-free, allowing the fund to retain the full proceeds.

Summary of Tax Strategy

- **One-Third CGT Discount:** Reduces CGT liability to an effective rate of 10% on properties held for more than 12 months in the accumulation phase.
- **Tax-Free Capital Gains in Pension Phase:** No CGT on property sales once the SMSF enters the pension phase.
- **Timing the Sale:** Deferring property sales until the pension phase eliminates CGT.

3. Rental Income and Deductions

Rental income from property in an SMSF is taxed at concessional rates, but SMSFs can further reduce taxable income by claiming a variety of deductions related to the property.

a) Tax on Rental Income (Accumulation Phase)

Rental income in the accumulation phase is taxed at 15%, but SMSFs can reduce this by deducting:

- Property management fees;
- Interest on SMSF loans (Limited Recourse Borrowing Arrangements);
- Maintenance and repairs; and
- Insurance premiums.

These deductions help lower the SMSF's taxable income and reduce the tax burden.

- **Example:** If an SMSF earns $60,000 in rental income and incurs $20,000 in deductible expenses, the taxable rental income is reduced to $40,000. The SMSF will pay $6,000 in tax (15% of $40,000).

b) Tax-Free Rental Income in the Pension Phase

Once the SMSF moves into the pension phase, all rental income is tax-free, providing a substantial tax advantage for trustees using property investments to generate passive income in retirement.

- **Example:** An SMSF generating $50,000 in rental income in the pension phase pays no tax on this income.

4. Depreciation Deductions for Property Investments

Depreciation is a powerful tax mitigation strategy for property investors in an SMSF, as it allows trustees to reduce taxable income by claiming depreciation on the property and its fixtures.

a) Depreciation on Buildings

SMSFs can claim depreciation on properties built after 1987 under the capital works allowance, which allows for a 2.5% deduction per year over 40 years.

- **Example:** If the construction cost of the SMSF property was $300,000, the SMSF can claim an annual depreciation deduction of $7,500.

b) Depreciation on Fixtures and Fittings

SMSFs can also claim depreciation on items such as carpets, appliances, and air-conditioning systems, which typically have shorter depreciation schedules ranging from 5 to 15 years. By claiming depreciation on both the building and its fixtures, SMSFs can significantly reduce taxable rental income and overall tax liability.

Summary of Depreciation Deductions

- **Building Depreciation:** Annual deduction of 2.5% of the construction cost for properties built post-1987.
- **Fixtures and Fittings:** Shorter depreciation schedules (5-15 years), reducing taxable rental income.

5. Limited Recourse Borrowing Arrangements (LRBAs) and Interest Deductions

Limited Recourse Borrowing Arrangements (LRBAs) allow SMSFs to borrow to purchase property, while limiting the lender's recourse to the specific property being acquired. One of the primary tax benefits of LRBAs is that the interest paid on the loan is tax-deductible, reducing the fund's taxable income.

a) Deducting Interest on Borrowings

Interest payments on LRBAs can be deducted from the SMSF's rental income, which significantly reduces the fund's taxable income in the accumulation phase.

- **Example:** If an SMSF earns $70,000 in rental income and pays $30,000 in interest on an LRBA, the taxable income is reduced to $40,000. The SMSF would pay $6,000 in tax (15% of $40,000).

b) PAYG Variations to Assist Loan Repayments

To help service SMSF loans, trustees can use PAYG (Pay-As-You-Go) tax variations to improve cash flow. PAYG variations allow trustees to reduce the amount of tax withheld from their salary, freeing up additional funds to contribute to the SMSF, which can then be used for loan repayments.

- **How it Works:** Trustees can apply to the ATO to vary their PAYG withholding based on their expected income and expenses for the year. By reducing the amount of tax withheld from their salary, trustees can increase their super contributions, which can then be used to repay the SMSF loan.
- **Example:** A trustee with significant interest expenses on an SMSF property loan can apply for a PAYG variation, reducing their withholding tax by $8,000 for the year. This extra $8,000 can then be contributed to the SMSF and used for loan repayments.

Summary of LRBA and PAYG Variations

- **Interest Deductions:** Deductible interest payments reduce taxable income, lowering the SMSF's tax liability.
- **PAYG Variations:** Reduces withholding tax, providing more funds for SMSF contributions and loan repayments.

6. Superannuation Contribution Caps for 2025-26

Superannuation contributions are a key component of SMSF tax efficiency. The 2025-26 superannuation contribution caps, as per current legislation, are as follows:

- **Concessional Contributions Cap:** $30,000 per year. These are pre-tax contributions, including employer contributions (such as the Superannuation Guarantee) and salary sacrifice. Concessional contributions are taxed at 15% when they enter the SMSF.

- **Non-Concessional Contributions Cap:** $120,000 per year. These contributions are made from after-tax income and are not taxed when they enter the SMSF. Individuals under 75 can access the bring-forward rule, which allows up to $360,000 to be contributed over three years.

Strategy: Trustees should aim to maximise concessional contributions up to the cap to reduce their personal tax liability while growing their SMSF's capital base for property investments.

Summary of Contribution Types

- **Concessional Contributions:** Taxed at 15% upon entry into the SMSF, capped at $30,000 for 2025-26.
- **Non-Concessional Contributions:** Not taxed when they enter the SMSF, capped at $120,000 for 2025-26.

Conclusion

SMSFs investing in property can take advantage of several tax efficiencies, from concessional tax rates to deductible expenses and interest. By managing rental income and capital gains tax effectively and utilising strategies like depreciation and PAYG variations, SMSFs can significantly reduce their tax liability and improve cash flow. Understanding the updated 2024-25 superannuation rates and thresholds ensures trustees maximise the tax benefits available within the SMSF structure.

In the next chapter, I will cover "Estate Planning and Succession Strategies for SMSFs", exploring how trustees can plan for a smooth transfer of SMSF assets to beneficiaries while minimising tax implications.

CHAPTER 8: Estate Planning and Succession Strategies for SMSFs

Estate planning within an SMSF is essential for ensuring that the fund's assets, including property, are passed on smoothly and tax-effectively to beneficiaries. Unlike other superannuation funds, SMSF trustees have direct control over the structure and transfer of assets. This chapter covers the key considerations and strategies for estate planning in an SMSF, focusing on how to minimise tax implications, avoid disputes, and ensure compliance with relevant superannuation laws.

1. The Importance of Estate Planning in an SMSF

Estate planning in an SMSF involves ensuring that the fund's assets are distributed according to the trustee's wishes upon their death. Without a clear and legally sound plan in place, SMSF assets, including property, may not be passed on in a way that aligns with the trustee's intentions. In particular, property investments in an SMSF need careful planning to ensure their efficient transfer, especially as property can be difficult to liquidate or divide among multiple beneficiaries.

Key Reasons for Estate Planning

- **Control Over Asset Distribution:** Proper planning ensures the SMSF trustee's assets, including property, are distributed according to their wishes.
- **Minimising Tax:** Without planning, beneficiaries may face significant tax liabilities, especially on taxable components of superannuation.
- **Avoiding Disputes:** Clear documentation helps prevent family disputes or legal challenges, ensuring a smoother transfer of assets.

2. SMSF Death Benefits: What Happens When a Member Dies

Upon the death of an SMSF member, the remaining trustees (or corporate trustee) are responsible for distributing the deceased's death benefits to their nominated beneficiaries. The death benefits typically include the member's account balance, which consists of contributions, earnings, and property or other investments held by the SMSF.

a) Death Benefit Nominations

A death benefit nomination is a formal instruction provided by the SMSF member, specifying who should receive their superannuation benefits upon their death. There are two types of nominations:

- ***Binding Death Benefit Nomination* (BDBN):** A BDBN ensures that the trustees must follow the member's instructions to distribute their superannuation to the nominated beneficiaries.
- ***Non-Binding Nomination:*** A non-binding nomination indicates the member's preference but gives the trustees discretion to decide how the benefits should be distributed.

Key Points to Consider:

- ***Reversionary Pension:*** For members receiving a pension, a reversionary pension allows the income stream to continue to a nominated beneficiary (typically a spouse) upon the member's death.
- **Validity of Nomination:** Trustees must ensure that nominations are valid and comply with SMSF rules. Binding nominations must be renewed regularly (typically every three years) unless they are specified as non-lapsing.

b) Eligible Beneficiaries

Under superannuation law, only certain individuals can be nominated as beneficiaries for death benefits. These typically include:

- Spouses (including de facto and same-sex partners);
- Children (including adult children);
- Financial dependents; and
- Individuals in an interdependent relationship with the member.

3. Tax Treatment of Death Benefits

One of the most critical aspects of estate planning in an SMSF is managing the tax implications of death benefits. The tax treatment of death benefits depends on the relationship between the deceased member and the beneficiary, as well as the type of benefit being paid (lump sum or income stream).

a) Lump Sum Payments

- ***Tax-Free Component:*** The *tax-free component* of a death benefit (generally made up of non-concessional contributions) is not subject to tax when paid to a beneficiary, regardless of their relationship to the deceased.
- ***Taxable Component:*** The *taxable component* (derived from concessional contributions and investment earnings) may be subject to tax, depending on the beneficiary:
    - **Death Benefit Paid to a Tax-Dependent:** Tax-dependents (such as spouses or children under 18) receive both the tax-free and taxable components of the death benefit tax-free.
    - **Death Benefit Paid to a Non-Tax-Dependent:** Non-tax dependents (such as adult children) are generally subject to tax on the taxable component at 15%, plus the Medicare levy.

b) Income Streams (Pensions)

If a death benefit is paid as a reversionary pension, the tax treatment depends on the age of the deceased and the beneficiary:

- **Deceased or Beneficiary Aged 60 or Over:** The pension payments are tax-free.
- **Both Aged Under 60:** The pension payments are taxable at the beneficiary's marginal tax rate, but they will become tax-free once the beneficiary turns 60.

Death Benefit Type	Tax Treatment
Lump Sum – Paid to a Tax-Dependent	Both taxable and tax-free components are tax-free.
Lump Sum – Paid to a Non-Dependent	Taxable component taxed at 15% + Medicare levy.
Reversionary Pension	Tax-free if either the deceased or beneficiary are aged 60 or over.

4. Succession Planning for SMSF Property

Property held in an SMSF can present unique challenges in estate planning, particularly because property cannot be easily divided among multiple beneficiaries. Careful planning is required to ensure that the property is either sold or transferred efficiently upon the death of a member.

a) Options for SMSF Property Upon Death

There are several options available for managing property assets upon the death of an SMSF member:

- **Sell the Property:** The SMSF may sell the property and distribute the proceeds to beneficiaries. If the property is sold during the pension phase, any capital gains will be tax-free.

- **Transfer Property to Beneficiaries:** In certain cases, the property itself can be transferred to a beneficiary as part of their death benefit. However, this can trigger stamp duty and Capital Gains Tax (CGT) if the SMSF is in the accumulation phase.
- **Continue Holding the Property:** If the property generates rental income, the SMSF may continue to hold the property and pay the rental income to beneficiaries via income streams (reversionary pensions).

b) Avoiding Liquidity Issues

One of the main concerns when leaving property in an SMSF is the liquidity required to pay out benefits to beneficiaries. If the property makes up a large portion of the fund's assets, the SMSF may struggle to meet its obligations without selling the property. To avoid liquidity problems:

- **Maintain Cash Reserves:** Trustees should ensure the SMSF has sufficient liquid assets to pay benefits without needing to sell property.
- **Use Insurance:** Life insurance policies held within the SMSF can provide cash benefits to beneficiaries, helping to avoid the forced sale of property assets.

Succession Options for SMSF Property

Succession Option	Details
Sell Property	Property sold, and proceeds distributed; CGT-free if in pension phase.
Transfer Property to Beneficiaries	Property transferred, but may trigger stamp duty and CGT if in accumulation phase.
Continue Holding Property	Property held, and rental income paid to beneficiaries via income streams.
Continue Holding Property	Property held, and rental income paid to beneficiaries via income streams.

5. Control of the SMSF Upon Death

One of the most critical aspects of estate planning in an SMSF is ensuring that the right people control the fund upon the death of a trustee. Inappropriately structured funds can lead to control issues, particularly if family disputes arise over the distribution of assets.

a) Appointing a Successor Trustee

To ensure the SMSF is managed according to the member's wishes after their death, it is essential to appoint a successor trustee or ensure that a corporate trustee structure is in place. A corporate trustee provides continuity and allows family members to retain control of the fund without the complexities of replacing individual trustees.

- ***Individual Trustee Structure:*** In an individual trustee structure, the remaining trustees must appoint a new trustee upon the death of a member. This can lead to disputes if the deceased member did not clearly indicate their successor trustee.

- ***Corporate Trustee Structure:*** A corporate trustee allows control of the SMSF to pass more smoothly, as the company continues as the trustee, and control can be passed to the next generation through shareholding or director appointments.

b) Ensuring Valid Estate Planning Documents

SMSF trustees should ensure that their estate planning documents are in order, including:

- Updated trust deeds;
- Binding Death Benefit Nominations (BDBNs); and
- Wills that clearly align with SMSF rules and superannuation laws.

Conclusion

Estate planning and succession strategies are vital components of managing an SMSF, particularly when property is involved. By ensuring that clear death benefit nominations are in place, minimising tax on death benefits, and addressing property succession issues, trustees can ensure a smooth and tax-effective transfer of assets to beneficiaries. Planning ahead is essential to avoid liquidity issues and disputes, allowing the SMSF to meet its long-term goals.

Reference Section for SMSF Estate Planning

1. **Binding Death Benefit Nominations (BDBNs):** Ensure that beneficiaries are clearly nominated, and the nominations are legally binding.
2. **Death Benefit Taxation:** Lump sums are tax-free for dependents; non-dependents may be taxed at 15% + Medicare levy on taxable components.
3. ***Reversionary Pension:*** A reversionary pension allows a surviving spouse or dependent to continue receiving the deceased's pension.

CHAPTER 9: Transitioning to Retirement and Pension Strategies in an SMSF

As SMSF members approach retirement, transitioning the fund from the accumulation phase to the pension phase becomes a critical step. This transition allows the SMSF to benefit from the **tax-free pension phase**, where investment earnings, including rental income from property and capital gains, are exempt from tax. Proper planning ensures that the SMSF is able to generate enough income to support retirement goals, while also taking full advantage of the tax concessions available.

This chapter covers key pension strategies for SMSFs, including how to structure property investments for retirement income, how to use the **$2 million transfer balance cap** effectively, and how to manage the minimum pension requirements.

1. Understanding the Transition to Retirement (TTR)

The **Transition to Retirement (TTR)** strategy allows SMSF members to start drawing a pension from their super while continuing to work, typically from age **55** (if commenced earlier) or **60**. This strategy is useful for members who want to gradually reduce their working hours while supplementing their income with pension payments from their SMSF.

a) Transition to Retirement Income Stream (TRIS)

A **Transition to Retirement Income Stream (TRIS)** enables SMSF members to start accessing their superannuation in the form of a pension before fully retiring. Under TRIS, the fund continues to be taxed at **15%** on its earnings, but members can withdraw up to **10%** of their super balance each year as income.

TRIS Restrictions: Members cannot withdraw lump sums while in a TRIS unless they meet a condition of release (such as reaching age 65 or retiring). However, pension payments can provide a valuable income stream during the transition phase.

Using TRIS with Property: For SMSFs holding property, TRIS allows rental income from the property to be used for regular pension payments to members, creating a smooth income stream while maintaining property ownership in the fund.

b) Full Retirement or Reaching Age 65

Once members either **retire** or reach age **65**, the SMSF transitions fully into the **pension phase**, where the fund's earnings and capital gains become **tax-free**. This is a significant advantage for property-rich SMSFs, as rental income and capital gains from the sale of property are no longer subject to tax.

2. The Pension Phase: Tax-Free Income and Capital Gains

The pension phase offers substantial tax benefits for SMSFs. Once the SMSF enters this phase, all earnings, including rental income from property and capital gains, become tax-free, provided the member's pension balance remains within the **$1.9 million transfer balance cap**.

a) Tax-Free Rental Income from Property

In the pension phase, rental income from SMSF-owned property is completely **tax-free**. This makes property an attractive asset for SMSFs focused on generating a reliable income stream during retirement.

Example: If an SMSF receives $50,000 in annual rental income from a residential property, that income is **tax-free** in the pension phase, providing a stable, inflation-adjusted source of retirement income.

b) Tax-Free Capital Gains on Property Sales

Another significant benefit of the pension phase is that any capital gains realised from the sale of property are **exempt from CGT**. This creates an opportunity for trustees to realize gains on property investments without incurring tax liabilities, maximising the value of the asset for members.

Example: An SMSF sells a commercial property for a capital gain of $600,000 while in the pension phase. Since the fund is in pension mode, the entire capital gain is **tax-free**, significantly increasing the proceeds that can be used for member benefits or reinvested in the fund.

c) The $2 Million Transfer Balance Cap (2025-26)

The **transfer balance cap** sets the maximum amount that an individual can transfer into a tax-free pension account. For 2024-25, this cap is **$2 million** per member. Any amount above this cap must remain in the accumulation phase, where earnings are taxed at 15%.

Maximising the Cap: To take full advantage of the pension phase tax exemptions, trustees should aim to maximize their pension balance up to the $2 million cap. Couples can jointly hold up to **$4 million** across their SMSF pension accounts, allowing for significant tax-free growth on both property income and other assets.

Accumulation Balances: If an SMSF has a property that exceeds the transfer balance cap, the portion above the cap will remain in the accumulation phase and continue to be taxed at **15%**. This allows the fund to maintain some concessional tax treatment, even for assets that exceed the cap.

Tax Advantages in the Pension Phase	Details
Tax-Free Rental Income	All rental income from SMSF property becomes tax-free once in the pension phase.
Tax-Free Capital Gains	Capital gains on property sales are completely tax-exempt in the pension phase.
$1.9 Million Transfer Balance Cap	Income and gains up to this balance cap are tax-free; excess remains in accumulation and is taxed at 15%.

3. Meeting Minimum Pension Payment Requirements

Once an SMSF enters the pension phase, trustees must ensure they meet the **minimum pension payment requirements**. The minimum amount to be paid depends on the member's age and their total balance in the pension phase.

a) Minimum Pension Payment Rates (2025-26)

For 2025-26, the minimum pension payment rates are based on the member's age. These are calculated as a percentage of the member's pension balance:

Under 65: 4% of the pension balance.

65-74: 5% of the pension balance.

75-79: 6% of the pension balance.

80-84: 7% of the pension balance.

85-89: 9% of the pension balance.

Example: If an SMSF member aged 70 has a pension balance of $1.5 million, the minimum pension payment for the year is **$75,000** (5% of $1.5 million). Rental income from property can help meet this requirement.

b) Ensuring Sufficient Liquidity

To meet these minimum pension payment requirements, the SMSF must have sufficient liquidity. For SMSFs with substantial property holdings, it's essential that the fund generates enough rental income or holds liquid assets such as cash or shares to cover these payments.

Rental Income as Pension Payments: SMSFs that generate rental income from property can use that income to make pension payments, ensuring the fund meets its obligations without selling long-term assets.

Diversification for Liquidity: Holding other liquid assets, such as shares, bonds, or cash reserves, ensures the SMSF can meet pension payments if rental income is insufficient or inconsistent.

4. Property and Pension Phase: Strategic Considerations

For SMSFs with significant property holdings, managing these assets effectively during the pension phase is crucial. Trustees must ensure the property generates sufficient income and decide when, or if, to sell the property for capital gains.

a) Retaining Property for Long-Term Income

Many SMSF trustees opt to retain property during the pension phase because it provides a steady, inflation-adjusted income stream. Rental income can be used to meet pension payments while maintaining the capital growth potential of the property over time.

Inflation Hedge: Property, particularly rental properties, tends to keep pace with inflation, ensuring that the SMSF's income stream remains valuable over time.

Lower Volatility: Compared to other asset classes like equities or cryptocurrency, property tends to experience lower price volatility, making it a stable source of income in retirement.

b) Selling Property for Capital Gains

For SMSFs that hold property with significant unrealized capital gains, the pension phase offers an opportunity to sell property **tax-free** and realize those gains. Trustees may choose to sell properties to rebalance the portfolio or generate liquidity for member benefits.

Timing the Sale: Selling property in the pension phase ensures that any capital gains are exempt from tax. Trustees should plan property sales carefully to take full advantage of this exemption.

Reinvesting Proceeds: Once a property is sold, trustees can reinvest the proceeds into more liquid or income-generating assets, such as dividend-paying shares or fixed-income investments, to provide ongoing support for the pension payments.

Property Strategies in the Pension Phase	Details
Retaining Property for Rental Income	SMSFs can retain property for long-term rental income, which becomes tax-free in the pension phase.
Selling Property for Tax-Free Capital Gains	Property can be sold in the pension phase without incurring CGT, providing liquidity or funds for reinvestment.
Timing Sales to Maximize Benefits	Trustees should plan the timing of property sales to coincide with the pension phase for maximum tax efficiency.

5. Structuring Income Streams for Retirement

In addition to property, SMSF trustees can structure income streams from other assets, such as shares, bonds, or fixed-income investments. A well-structured income stream helps ensure that the fund can meet ongoing obligations without sacrificing long-term growth.

a) Combining Property and Other Income Streams

A diversified portfolio, including both property and other assets, ensures a stable income flow during retirement. For example, SMSFs can combine rental income with dividend payments from shares or interest from bonds, creating a more balanced and reliable income stream.

Diversified Income: By diversifying income sources, trustees reduce the risk of relying solely on one type of investment for pension payments.

b) Planning for Longevity

Trustees must ensure that the SMSF has enough assets to support members throughout their retirement, potentially for decades. Property, with its capital growth and rental income potential, plays a key role in providing for long-term financial security, especially when combined with other stable income-generating assets.

Conclusion

Transitioning to retirement is a crucial phase for SMSF members, and properly managing this transition ensures that the fund remains tax-efficient and capable of meeting pension obligations. Property plays a vital role in this transition, providing both rental income and tax-free capital gains in the pension phase. By understanding the tax advantages of the **$1.9 million transfer balance cap**, meeting minimum pension payment requirements, and strategically managing property assets, trustees can ensure their SMSF continues to support members throughout their retirement.

Reference Section for Transition to Retirement and Pension Strategies

Transition to Retirement Income Stream (TRIS): Allows SMSF members to draw a pension while still working, taxed at 15% on earnings.

$2 Million Transfer Balance Cap: Limits the amount transferred to a tax-free pension account; excess remains in accumulation.

Minimum Pension Payment Rates (2025-26): Pension payments are a percentage of the member's balance, starting at 4% for those under 65.

CHAPTER 10: SMSF Exit Strategies and SMSF Wind Up

As SMSF members approach retirement, transitioning the fund from the accumulation phase to the pension phase becomes a critical step. This transition allows the SMSF to benefit from the tax-free pension phase, where investment earnings, including rental income from property and capital gains, are exempt from tax. Proper planning ensures that the SMSF is able to generate enough income to support retirement goals; while also taking full advantage of the tax concessions available.

This chapter covers key pension strategies for SMSFs, including how to structure property investments for retirement income, how to use the $1.9 million transfer balance cap effectively, and how to manage the minimum pension requirements.

1. Understanding the Transition to Retirement (TTR)

The *Transition to Retirement* (TTR) strategy allows SMSF members to start drawing a pension from their super while continuing to work, typically upon reaching their preservation age (currently 60). This strategy is useful for members who want to gradually reduce their working hours while supplementing their income with pension payments from their SMSF.

2. Strategic Approaches to Property in Retirement

a) Selling Property Before Retirement (Accumulation Phase)

During the accumulation phase, when trustees are still working and making contributions to their SMSF, selling property may be necessary to rebalance the fund or improve liquidity. If the property is sold while the SMSF is still in this phase, any capital gains are subject to tax at the concessional rate of 15%. If the property has been held for more than 12 months, the capital gains tax (CGT) is reduced to 10% due to the one-third CGT discount.

- **Advantages:** Selling before retirement provides the SMSF with capital to diversify into other investments and boost liquidity, which can be used to generate passive income.
- **Disadvantages:** Selling during the accumulation phase results in a CGT liability, reducing the net proceeds from the sale.

b) Selling Property in the Pension Phase

One of the most significant advantages of holding property in an SMSF is the tax-free environment available once the fund enters the pension phase. If the SMSF sells property during this phase, any capital gains are completely tax-free, provided the property is held within the pension fund and all relevant limits (such as transfer balance caps) are observed.

- **Advantages:** No capital gains tax applies when selling property in the pension phase, maximising the proceeds from the sale.
- **Disadvantages:** The SMSF may need to maintain liquidity to pay out pensions, which can limit the timing of the sale.

c) Leasing Property for Ongoing Retirement Income

In some cases, trustees may decide not to sell the property at all, choosing instead to keep the property within the SMSF and rely on rental income to fund retirement. This strategy works particularly well for commercial properties or residential properties with stable, long-term tenants.

- **Advantages:** Retaining the property allows the SMSF to benefit from a steady rental income, which can be tax-free in the pension phase.

- **Disadvantages:** Maintaining a rental property requires ongoing management and incurs costs for upkeep, insurance, and property management. Trustees must also have the capacity to continue managing the fund.

d) Transfer of Property to Fund Members or Beneficiaries

Rather than selling property to a third party, trustees may choose to transfer ownership of the SMSF property to one or more fund members as part of their retirement benefits, or to beneficiaries as a death benefit. This approach requires careful planning to avoid breaching contribution caps or triggering excessive tax liabilities.

- **Advantages:** The property remains in the family or among fund members, and the transfer can be structured to minimise tax implications. It also avoids the need to find a buyer in the open market.

- **Disadvantages:** Transferring property can be complex, and valuation, stamp duty, and legal costs may apply. CGT may also apply if the transfer occurs during the accumulation phase.

3. Managing Capital Gains Tax (CGT) on SMSF Property Sales

CGT is one of the most important factors to consider when selling property within an SMSF. The tax treatment of capital gains depends on whether the SMSF is in the accumulation phase or pension phase at the time of the sale.

CGT in the Accumulation Phase

When an SMSF sells property during the accumulation phase, any capital gains are taxed at 15%. If the property has been held for more than 12 months, the SMSF qualifies for a one-third CGT discount, reducing the effective CGT rate to 10%.

Example: If the SMSF sells a property that was purchased for $500,000 and is now worth $800,000, the capital gain would be $300,000. With the one-third discount, the taxable gain would be $200,000, and the SMSF would pay $30,000 in CGT (15% of the $200,000 taxable gain, which is effectively 10% of the $300,000 gross gain).

CGT in the Pension Phase

Once the SMSF enters the pension phase, any capital gains on the sale of property are completely tax-free. This makes it advantageous for trustees to hold onto property until they reach the pension phase, maximising the value of the sale without incurring CGT.

Example: Using the same scenario, if the SMSF sells the property after entering the pension phase, the $300,000 capital gain would be tax-free, allowing the full proceeds of $800,000 to remain in the fund.

4. Timing the Sale: Market Conditions and SMSF Needs

The decision to sell SMSF property should take into account market conditions and the fund's liquidity needs. Selling in a high-growth market can maximise proceeds, while selling during a downturn may lock in lower gains or even result in losses. Trustees should also consider SMSF's overall investment strategy and whether selling the property aligns with long-term goals.

a) Selling in a Growth Market

If the property market is experiencing strong capital growth, selling the property can generate significant profits for the SMSF. However, trustees must consider whether the SMSF will be able to replace this growth with other investments that can generate similar returns.

b) Selling in a Declining Market

In a downturn, it may be more beneficial to hold onto the property and wait for the market to recover. Selling during a market decline can result in lower returns, and the SMSF may not be able to recover the losses through other investments. However, if the fund is being wound up or liquidity is urgently needed, waiting may not be an option.

5. Compliance Considerations When Selling Property in an SMSF

Selling property within an SMSF involves a number of compliance obligations that trustees must observe. These include ensuring that the sale is conducted at arm's length and that the proceeds are used appropriately in line with the *Sole Purpose Test* (SIS Act Section 62), which requires that the fund be maintained solely to provide retirement benefits for its members.

a) Arm's Length Transactions

The *Arm's Length Rule* (SIS Act Section 109) requires that all property transactions within an SMSF are conducted at market value and on commercial terms. If the SMSF sells property to a related party, the price must be supported by an independent valuation to avoid penalties.

b) Maintaining the Sole Purpose Test

When selling property, trustees must ensure that the proceeds are used in line with the *Sole Purpose Test.* This means that the funds generated from the sale should be used to benefit the members' retirement savings, whether through reinvestment or distribution as part of a pension.

6. Property Sale Costs and Fees

Selling property involves various costs that trustees must account for when planning their exit strategy. These costs can reduce the net proceeds from the sale, so it's essential to include them in the overall planning.

- **Real Estate Agent Fees:** Typically range from 1.5% to 3% of the sale price.
- **Legal Fees:** Legal services for the sale of property, including contract preparation and conveyancing, can add additional costs.
- **Capital Gains Tax (CGT):** As discussed, CGT applies in the accumulation phase but can be avoided in the pension phase.
- **Valuation Costs:** An independent valuation may be required to establish market value, especially if selling to a related party.

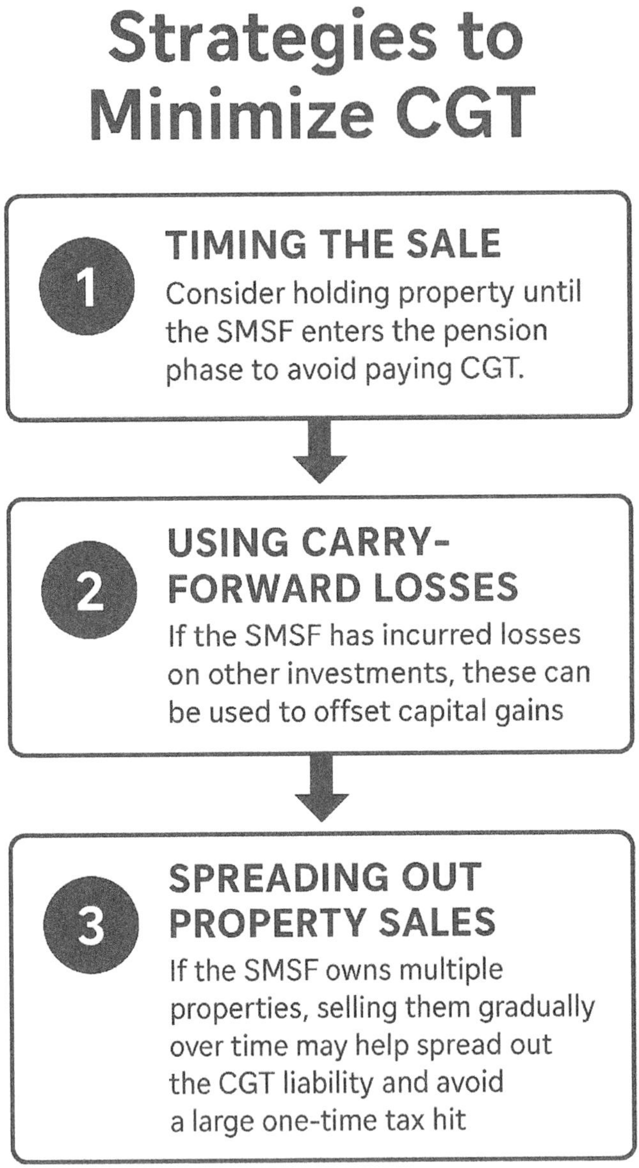
Strategies to Minimize CGT
1
TIMING THE SALE
Consider holding property until the SMSF enters the pension phase to avoid paying CGT.
2
USING CARRY-FORWARD LOSSES
If the SMSF has incurred losses on other investments, these can be used to offset capital gains
3
SPREADING OUT PROPERTY SALES
If the SMSF owns multiple properties, selling them gradually over time may help spread out the CGT liability and avoid a large one-time tax hit

7. Reasons for Winding Up an SMSF

While the strategies above focus on selling property while the SMSF continues operating, there may come a time when trustees need to wind up the fund entirely. This could happen for several reasons, and understanding these situations helps trustees recognise when it is time to close the fund and start planning the process.

a) Death of All Members

One of the most common reasons for winding up an SMSF is when all members have passed away, and the fund no longer has any beneficiaries to provide for. In this case, trustees must ensure that the fund's assets are distributed according to the members' death benefit nominations and the provisions of the trust deed.

b) Costs Outweigh Benefits

As members age and their super balances decline, the costs associated with running an SMSF (such as accounting, audit fees, and administrative costs) may outweigh the benefits of maintaining the fund. In such cases, trustees may opt to wind up the SMSF and roll over the remaining balance into a retail or industry super fund.

Example: If an SMSF has declining balances but the annual fees remain fixed at $3,000-$5,000, the administrative burden may become too costly to justify maintaining the fund, particularly if the balance has fallen below $200,000.

c) Loss of Capacity to Manage the SMSF

If the trustees lose the ability to manage the SMSF (due to age, illness, or mental incapacity), winding up the fund may be necessary. Alternatively, a corporate trustee or professional fund administrator can be appointed to manage the fund, but in some cases, it may be simpler to close the SMSF.

d) Members No Longer Wish to Manage the Fund

Some members may no longer want the responsibility of managing an SMSF, particularly as they approach retirement or wish to simplify their

Reasons for Winding Up an SMSF

	Details
Death of All Members	Trustees must distribute death benefits and close the fund.
Costs Outweigh Benefits	Ongoing costs may become too high relative to the fund's balance.
Loss of Capacity	Trustees may lose the capacity to manage the fund, leading to winding up.
Members No Longer Wish to Manage the Fund	Members may prefer to roll over their balance into a managed super fund

financial affairs. In these cases, members may choose to wind up the fund and transfer their superannuation to a managed super fund that offers less hands-on involvement.

8. Liquidating SMSF Assets When Winding Up

If an SMSF holds property or other significant assets, trustees must manage the sale or transfer of these investments when winding up the fund. The strategy for liquidating assets depends on the type of investments held, the tax implications of selling assets, and whether the SMSF is in the accumulation phase or pension phase.

a) Selling or Transferring Property

When winding up an SMSF that holds property, trustees may choose to sell the property or transfer it to a beneficiary. The decision depends on the specific circumstances of the fund and the beneficiaries' preferences.

- **Selling Property:** Apply the same CGT rules discussed earlier: 15% (or 10% with discount) in the accumulation phase, tax-free in the pension phase.
- **Transferring Property to Beneficiaries:** The SMSF may transfer property directly to a beneficiary as part of their lump sum death benefit or final benefit payment. This option may avoid the need to sell the property, but trustees must ensure that any stamp duty or legal transfer fees are accounted for.

b) Liquidating Other Investments

Other SMSF investments, such as shares, bonds, and managed funds, must also be liquidated or transferred to beneficiaries. Trustees should consider the market value of these assets and any capital gains that may apply upon liquidation.

- **Liquidating Shares:** Capital gains are taxed at 15% (or 10% with the one-third CGT discount) in the accumulation phase, but tax-free during the pension phase.
- **Rollover to Managed Super Fund:** If members choose to roll over their remaining superannuation into a managed fund, the SMSF assets must first be liquidated and the cash balance transferred to the new fund. No CGT applies to amounts rolled over into a regulated super fund.

Asset Liquidation Options	Details
Selling Property	Capital gains are taxed at 15% (or 10% with discount) in accumulation and are tax-free in the pension phase.
Transferring Property	Property can be transferred to beneficiaries, but stamp duty and legal fees may apply.
Liquidating Shares/Other Investments	CGT applies in the accumulation phase, but gains are tax-free in the pension phase.
Rollover to Managed Fund	No CGT applies to amounts rolled over into a regulated super fund.

9. Paying Out Member Benefits

When winding up an SMSF, trustees must ensure that all member benefits are distributed before the fund is closed. The method of paying out benefits depends on the members' circumstances, including whether they are still working or retired.

a) Lump Sum Payments

For members who have met a condition of release (such as reaching retirement age or permanent incapacity), benefits can be paid as a lump sum. Lump sums paid from the tax-free component of the SMSF are not taxed, while the taxable component may be subject to tax unless the member is over age 60.

Example: A member aged 65 receives a lump sum payment from their SMSF, consisting of a $1 million tax-free component and a $500,000 taxable component. As the member is over 60, no tax is payable on either component.

b) Rollovers to Other Super Funds

For members who have not yet met a condition of release or wish to continue managing their super, benefits can be rolled over into another regulated super fund, such as a retail or industry fund. This ensures that the member's superannuation continues to grow in a tax-advantaged environment.

- **No Tax on Rollovers:** When rolling over benefits to another superannuation fund, there is no tax liability on the amount transferred. However, trustees must ensure that all assets are liquidated before making the rollover.

c) Death Benefit Payments to Beneficiaries

If a member has passed away, their superannuation must be distributed according to their death benefit nomination. Beneficiaries may receive the benefits as a lump sum or, in the case of a reversionary pension, as an ongoing income stream. The tax treatment of death benefits depends on whether the recipient is a tax dependent or non-tax dependent.

- **Tax Dependent Recipients:** If a death benefit is paid to a tax dependent (such as a spouse or minor child), it is generally tax-free.
- **Non-Tax Dependent Recipients:** If paid to a non-tax dependent (such as an adult child), the taxable component is subject to tax at 15% plus the Medicare levy.

Member Benefit Payment Options

Member Benefit Payment Options	Details
Lump Sum Payments	Lump sums are tax-free for members over 60; taxable components are taxed otherwise.
Rollovers to Other Super Funds	No tax applies on rollovers to another regulated superannuation fund.
Death Benefit Payments	Tax-free for tax dependants; non-tax dependants are taxed at 15% plus the Medicare levy on the taxable component.

10. Final Steps to Wind Up the SMSF

Once all assets have been sold or transferred and member benefits have been paid out, trustees can take the final steps to wind up the SMSF. This involves completing the necessary administrative and reporting tasks to officially close the fund.

a) Notify the ATO

The first step in winding up the SMSF is to minute this step and then rollover super to your new super funds. Next, complete the funds final return where the Australian Taxation Office (ATO) notified.

Final Audit: Before the SMSF can be wound up, a final audit must be conducted. This audit reviews the fund's financial records and ensures that all tax obligations have been met.

b) Close Bank Accounts and Cancel ABN

Once the final audit is complete and the ATO has been notified in the final return, trustees must close the SMSF's bank accounts and cancel the fund's Australian Business Number (ABN) and GST registration, if applicable. Any remaining funds in the SMSF's bank accounts should be distributed to members or rolled over into another super fund before the accounts are closed.

- **Bank Account Closure:** Ensure that no payments are outstanding before closing the SMSF bank account, as this may delay the winding-up process.

c) Keep Records for Five Years

Even after the SMSF has been wound up, trustees are required to retain all records related to the fund for at least five years. This includes financial statements, tax returns, audit reports, and records of all asset sales and benefit payments.

- **Compliance Check:** Keeping these records ensures that trustees can demonstrate compliance with ATO regulations if required in the future.

Final Steps to Wind Up the SMSF	Key Actions
Minute Decision submit Final Annual Return and Notify the ATO and	Minute the decision to wind up the SMSF. Complete the funds last return, roll out all monies to a new retail or Industry fund. Inform the ATO and submit an ABN cancellation form.
ABN cancellation letter - Close Bank Accounts	once the ABN cancellation letter is received from the ATO Ensure all accounts are closed
Keep Records for Five Years	Retain all SMSF records for a minimum of five years post-wind-up.

Conclusion

Developing a comprehensive exit strategy for SMSF property investments and understanding when to wind up the fund entirely are essential for trustees at various stages of their retirement journey. Whether selling property while the fund continues operating, leasing it for rental income, transferring it to fund members, or liquidating all assets as part of a complete fund wind-up, careful planning ensures tax efficiency and compliance with SMSF regulations.

Timing the sale to take advantage of the tax-free environment in the pension phase can significantly maximise returns for fund members. Understanding the CGT implications, managing compliance requirements, and knowing when the costs or circumstances warrant winding up the fund will ensure a smooth transition into retirement or a compliant fund closure.

By following the strategies outlined in this chapter, trustees can make informed decisions that align with their retirement goals, minimise tax liabilities, and meet all regulatory obligations throughout the exit process.

Reference Section for SMSF Exit Strategies

1. **Sole Purpose Test (SIS Act Section 62):** Ensures that all proceeds from property sales and fund operations are used for the benefit of fund members' retirement.
2. **Capital Gains Tax Rules:** CGT applies at 15% during the accumulation phase, with a one-third discount (effective rate of 10%) for property held over 12 months, and is tax-free in the pension phase.
3. **Arm's Length Rule (SIS Act Section 109):** Requires that property sales, especially those involving related parties, are conducted at market value with proper documentation.
4. **ATO Winding-Up Procedures:** Trustees must notify the ATO when winding up an SMSF and submit the final annual return with a completed audit.
5. **Death Benefit Payments:** Lump sums paid to tax dependants are tax-free; non-tax dependants may be taxed at 15% plus the Medicare levy on the taxable component.

CHAPTER 11: Ongoing SMSF Compliance and Investment Management

Running an SMSF comes with ongoing responsibilities, including ensuring compliance with Australian Taxation Office (ATO) regulations, maintaining the fund's investment strategy, and managing property and other assets effectively. Trustees must continuously monitor the fund's performance and ensure that it adheres to the *Superannuation Industry (Supervision) Act 1993* (SIS Act), as non-compliance can result in severe penalties. In this chapter, I will explore key compliance obligations and strategies for managing SMSF investments to maximise returns while staying within regulatory guidelines.

1. SMSF Compliance Requirements: Staying on Track

SMSFs are subject to strict compliance obligations set out by the ATO and regulated under the SIS Act. Failure to meet these requirements can result in the fund being deemed non-compliant, which can lead to significant tax penalties. Trustees need to be aware of the key compliance tasks to ensure their SMSF continues to enjoy its concessional tax status.

a) Investment Strategy Compliance

The investment strategy is a fundamental document that outlines how the SMSF will invest its assets to meet the retirement goals of its members under Regulation 4.09A. Trustees must regularly review and update the investment strategy to reflect changes in the fund's circumstances, the financial markets, or the needs of the members.

- **Key Considerations:** The investment strategy should consider risk tolerance, liquidity needs, and diversification. For example, if the SMSF is heavily invested in property, trustees may need to ensure there is sufficient liquidity to meet ongoing obligations such as loan repayments or pension payments.
- **Review Frequency:** The ATO requires that the investment strategy be reviewed annually or whenever there is a significant change in the fund's circumstances, such as the purchase of a large asset like property, or a member entering the pension phase.

b) Valuing SMSF Assets

It is essential that trustees accurately value SMSF assets at market value, particularly when it comes to property and other illiquid investments. The ATO requires that SMSF assets be valued annually to ensure that the fund's financial statements are accurate and that members' balances are correctly reported.

- **Property Valuations:** For property investments, trustees should obtain a qualified property valuation at least every three years and an online valuation each year showing comparison pricing for similar properties in the region, or more frequently if the property market fluctuates significantly. This ensures that the SMSF's accounts reflect the true value of the property and helps with decision-making regarding rental income, property sales, or borrowing strategies.

c) Audits and Reporting

Each year, the SMSF must be audited by an independent SMSF auditor. The annual audit covers both the fund's financial statements and its compliance with superannuation laws. Trustees are also required to submit an Annual Return to the ATO, which includes financial information about the fund's income, expenses, and investments.

- **Audit Preparation:** Trustees should ensure all records, including rental agreements, bank statements, and property valuations, are up-to-date and available for the auditor. Good record-keeping helps avoid delays and ensures the audit process goes smoothly.

Compliance Task	Key Points
Reviewing Investment Strategy	Review annually or when there is a significant change in the fund.
Valuing SMSF Assets	Ensure accurate market valuations, particularly for property investments.
Annual Audit	Prepare for the annual audit by ensuring all records are up to date.

2. Managing Property Investments in an SMSF

Property investments often form a significant part of SMSF portfolios due to their long-term capital growth potential and income generation. However, managing property within an SMSF requires attention to several key areas, including maintaining liquidity, managing rental income, and ensuring ongoing compliance with borrowing rules.

a) Maintaining Liquidity

Liquidity is a critical issue for SMSFs with substantial property investments, as property is an illiquid asset. Trustees must ensure there is sufficient liquidity in the fund to meet ongoing obligations such as:

- **Loan Repayments:** For SMSFs with property purchased through a *Limited Recourse Borrowing Arrangement* (LRBA), the fund must maintain enough liquidity to service loan repayments.
- **Pension Payments:** Once a member reaches retirement and begins drawing a pension, the SMSF must ensure it can meet minimum pension payment requirements without having to sell property.

Strategies to Maintain Liquidity:

- **Diversify into Liquid Assets:** In addition to property, trustees should ensure the SMSF holds liquid assets such as cash, bonds, or equities to cover short-term liabilities.
- **Rental Income:** Ensure that rental income is sufficient to cover property-related expenses and contribute to the fund's overall liquidity.

b) Property Maintenance and Expenses

Trustees are responsible for managing property maintenance and ensuring that the property continues to generate rental income. Property-related expenses such as repairs, insurance, and management fees must be paid from the SMSF.

- **Deductibility of Expenses:** Most property-related expenses, such as maintenance, repairs, and insurance, are tax-deductible for the SMSF. This reduces the fund's taxable income and enhances tax efficiency.

c) Managing Borrowing through LRBAs

If the SMSF has used an LRBA (limited recourse borrowing arrangement) to purchase property, it's essential to comply with the borrowing rules set out by the SIS Act Sections 67A and 67B. LRBAs must be structured carefully, as the loan is limited to the specific property, and the lender has no recourse to the SMSF's other assets.

- **Repayment Strategy:** Trustees should ensure that the SMSF can comfortably service the loan through rental income and super contributions. PAYG variations can help free up cash flow to contribute to the fund for loan repayments.

3. Diversification and Risk Management

While property is a valuable asset class, SMSFs must also focus on diversification to spread risk across different investments. Having a well-diversified portfolio helps to protect the SMSF from market volatility in any one sector, including property.

a) Diversifying Across Asset Classes

A well-balanced SMSF portfolio typically includes a mix of property, shares, bonds, cash, and alternative investments. By diversifying into these asset classes, trustees can ensure that the SMSF is not over-exposed to any single risk.

- **Shares and Bonds:** Investing in shares provides capital growth potential, while bonds offer stability and fixed-income returns. Both asset classes provide liquidity, helping to balance the illiquid nature of property.

- **Cash Reserves:** Maintaining a cash buffer ensures that the SMSF can cover immediate expenses, including loan repayments and pension withdrawals, without having to sell long-term investments like property.

b) Risk Tolerance and Strategy Review

The SMSF's investment strategy must align with the members' risk tolerance and retirement goals. Over time, as members approach retirement, the fund may need to shift to a more conservative approach to preserve capital and ensure stable income.

- **Reviewing Risk Exposure:** Regularly reviewing the SMSF's investment performance and risk exposure is essential. Trustees should assess whether the portfolio still aligns with the fund's objectives and adjust the asset allocation as needed.

Investment Management	Strategies
Maintaining Liquidity	Ensure sufficient liquid assets to cover loan repayments and pension payments.
Diversification	Spread investments across property, shares, bonds, and cash for balanced risk.
Risk Management	Adjust asset allocation to align with risk tolerance and retirement goals.

4. Compliance with Superannuation Laws and Regulations

Staying compliant with superannuation laws and regulations is critical for maintaining the SMSF's tax-concessional status. Non-compliance can result in penalties, tax liabilities, or even disqualification of the fund.

a) Sole Purpose Test

The *Sole Purpose Test* (SIS Act Section 62) requires that SMSFs be maintained solely to provide retirement benefits for members. Property investments and other assets must be managed with this purpose in mind. Any personal use of SMSF assets, such as living in an SMSF-owned property, would breach this test and could result in penalties.

b) In-House Asset Rules

The *In-House Asset Rules* (SIS Act Section 71) limit the extent to which SMSFs can invest in assets linked to related parties. SMSFs are generally prohibited from investing more than 5% of the fund's total assets, in, in-house assets, which include loans to related parties or investments in entities controlled by members. Trustees must ensure that property and other investments comply with these rules.

c) Related Party Transactions and the Arm's Length Rule

SMSF property transactions must comply with the *Arm's Length Rule* (SIS Act Section 109), meaning that all transactions, including buying, selling, or leasing property, must be conducted at market value. Any favourable terms to a related party could breach superannuation rules and result in penalties.

- **Leasing Commercial Property to a Related Party:** SMSFs are allowed to lease business real property to a related party, provided the lease terms are at market rates and comply with the Arm's Length Rule.

Superannuation Compliance	Key Rules
Sole Purpose Test	SMSF must be maintained solely for providing retirement benefits.
In-House Asset Rules	Limits investment in related party assets to 5% of total fund assets.
Arm's Length Rule	All transactions must be conducted at market value.

Conclusion

Ongoing compliance and effective investment management are critical to the long-term success of an SMSF. Trustees must ensure that the fund's investment strategy aligns with members' retirement goals, while also maintaining liquidity and diversification to manage risk. By staying compliant with superannuation laws, including the Sole Purpose Test and Arm's Length Rule, and ensuring that property and other investments are managed effectively, trustees can optimise their SMSF for long-term financial security.

Reference Section for SMSF Compliance and Investment Management

Section 4.09A of SIS Regulations: Mandates the formulation and regular review of the SMSF's investment strategy, taking into account risk, diversification, liquidity, liabilities, and insurance.

1. **Sole Purpose Test (SIS Act Section 62):** Ensures the SMSF is maintained solely to provide retirement benefits for members.
2. **Arm's Length Rule (SIS Act Section 109):** Requires property transactions, including rental agreements, to be conducted at market value.

CHAPTER 12: Audit Requirements for SMSF Property Investments

Disclaimer

This chapter is educational. It summarises obligations under the SIS Act, SISR, and Australian Auditing Standards. It is not guidance. Trustees and practitioners should refer to legislation, ATO guidance, and professional standards for application to their circumstances.

1) Setting the Scene

Picture this: you and your partner have used your SMSF to buy a tidy investment property. Your regular super contributions and the rent quietly chip away at the loan while the property does what good assets do: grow. Then, like clockwork, 30 June comes and goes, and an independent auditor steps in for your fund's annual health check.

Contrary to urban legends, their job is not to trip you up. It is to protect your retirement savings by checking that the fund's financial statements present a fair view **(Part A)** and that the fund has followed the rules **(Part B).**

Property investments within SMSFs entail extra responsibility regarding title, valuation, lease, and bank evidence, which the ATO has reiterated recently. The idea is to have these documents ready before your auditor even asks.

Sole Purpose Test

The property must be held solely for providing retirement benefits.

Borrowing Rules

Where borrowing is involved, loan agreements must meet the strict rules for **limited recourse borrowing arrangements (LRBAs)**.

Related-Party Dealings

All transactions with related parties must be on **arm's length terms** in accordance with **SISA s109**.

Lease Documentation

Written lease agreements must be in place, supported by current **market rental evidence**.

Record-Keeping

Trustees must maintain accurate records of **rental income, property expenses, valuations, and loan repayment schedules**.

Important point: The SMSF that sails through audit isn't the one with perfect tenants or perfect timing. It's the one with predictable paperwork: the title search dated after year-end, a valuation backed by comparable sales, a signed lease with market-rate rent, and bank evidence to match.

2) What the Auditor Actually Does (and does not)

Audit Part	Purpose	Focus
Part A – Financial Report	Are the numbers right?	Market value at 30 June, rental income completeness, expenses, any LRBA balances, and disclosures.
Part B – Compliance	Did you follow the law?	**Sole purpose** (Section 62), arm's length (Section 109), borrowing rules (Section 67/LRBA), in-house assets (Section 71), investment strategy (Regulation 4.09), **prohibited charges** (Regulation 13.14).

Importantly, the auditor does not run your fund, or set your property's value. They test the evidence you provide. If evidence is missing or weak, they may need to modify their report and (if thresholds are met) lodge an Auditor Contravention Report (ACR) with the ATO.

3) Audit Process: from 1 July each year

These are the typically requested audit proofs:

- **Title search:** Dated after 30 June showing the correct trustee's name and no prohibited charges.
- **Valuation bundle:** Agent appraisal with at least two comparable sales, notes on improvements, and a quick check against local sales.
- **Lease agreement:** Signed, current; if it's a related-party lease, you've got a rental appraisal at commencement (or renewal).
- **Bank statements & rental statements:** Rent is paid in full and on time; expenses are fund-paid with invoices on file.
- **Investment strategy:** Updated for liquidity, diversification, and risk.

Your auditor's questions are faster to answer when your documents are pre-labelled and complete.

4) Ownership & Title Searches

New Annual Rule from 1 July 2025

What changed?
For each property, the auditor requires a title search dated close to the financial year-end (30 June).

Why it matters:

- **Confirms correct legal ownership** (corporate trustee or individual trustees "as trustee for the SMSF").
- **It confirms the current owner and who the lender is, and whether there are any charges against the**

property (demonstrating no prohibited charge over the asset under Regulation 13.14).

Without it, auditors may report a breach of Part B.

Trustee action: Order the title search immediately after 30 June; the report must be no older than 120 days.

5) Market Valuations: What "Good Evidence" Looks Like

The rule: Assets must be at market value at 30 June (Regulation 8.02B). The ATO expects objective, supportable evidence every year.

Time windows you can rely on:

- **Residential:** Valuation within 6 months of year-end.
- **Commercial:** Valuation within 12 months of year-end (supplement with rent rolls/yields where useful).

Acceptable evidence (mix and match, not just one source):

- Independent valuer's report;
- Real estate agent appraisal with comparable sales (at least two, recent);
- Recent arm's-length purchase price (if no material change);
- Details of improvements;
- Council rates (in support of the above);
- Yield analysis for commercial (in support of the above).

6) Leases & Rent: Related-Party and Market-Rate Proof

- A formal lease is required for every tenant (even when managed by an agent).
- If you truly cannot locate a lease, prepare a trustee minute setting out terms, but be aware that the auditor may still qualify Part A.

Related-party leases (e.g., your business as tenant):

- Obtain a rental appraisal at lease commencement (or renewal).
- **Below market:** Risk under Section 109 (Arm's Length Rule).
- **Above market:** Potential NALI exposure (punitive tax).

Rent evidence checklist:

- Bank statements showing timely, full payments;
- Rental invoices/manager statements;
- Rent reviews are documented in line with the lease.

7) Trustee Verification & Auditor Independence

- Trustees/directors must not be disqualified (ASIC search).
- Auditors must be independent (no reciprocal relationships, no in-house administration ties, and careful with very high volumes).
- Trustees should appoint an ASIC-registered auditor who is not otherwise servicing the fund's accounts/administration.

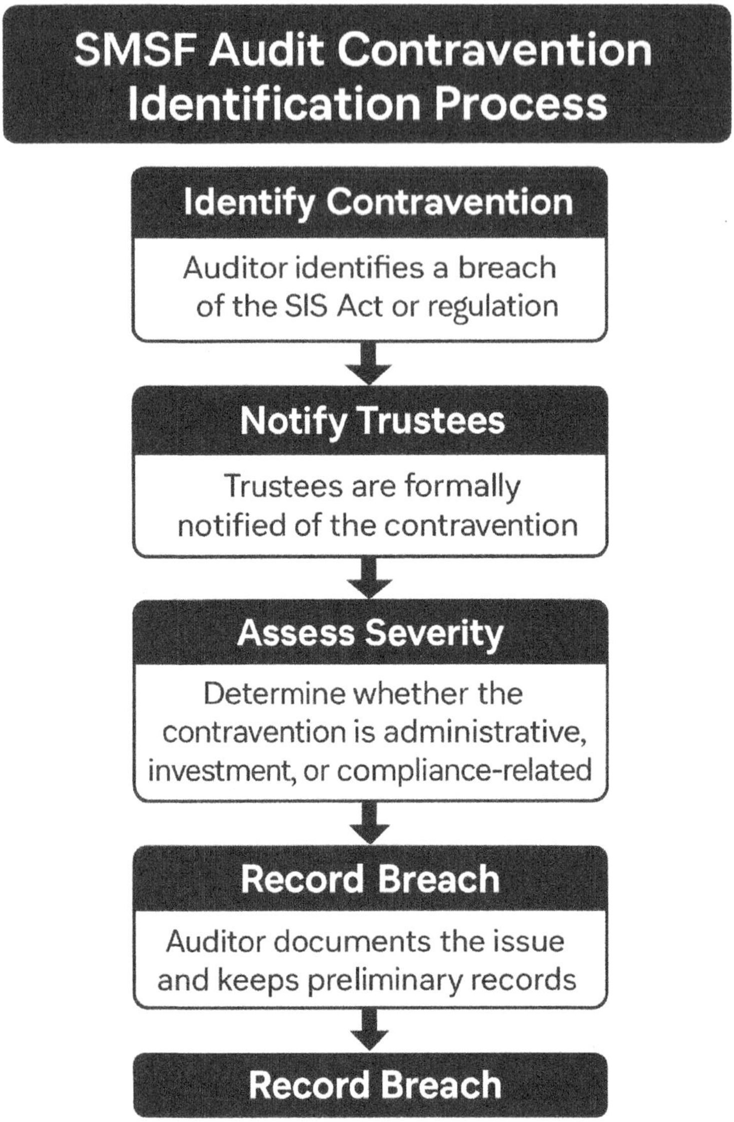
SMSF Audit Contravention Identification Process
Identify Contravention
Auditor identifies a breach of the SIS Act or regulation
Notify Trustees
Trustees are formally notified of the contravention
Assess Severity
Determine whether the contravention is administrative, investment, or compliance-related
Record Breach
Auditor documents the issue and keeps preliminary records
Record Breach

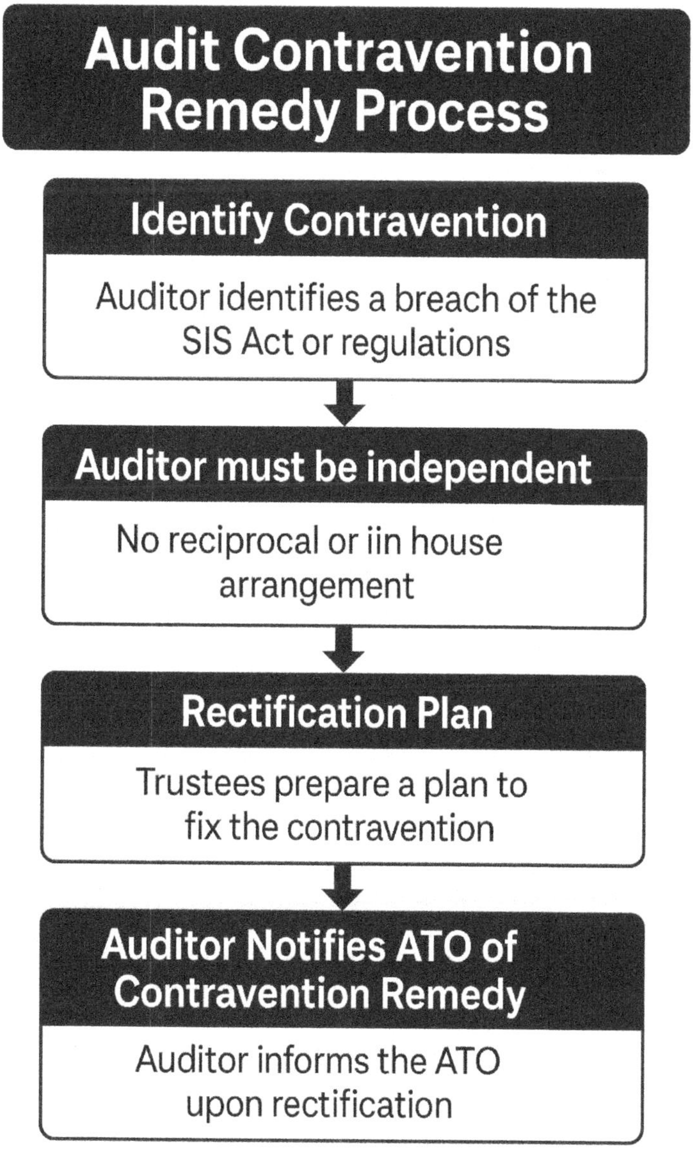
Audit Contravention Remedy Process
Identify Contravention
Auditor identifies a breach of the SIS Act or regulations
Auditor must be independent
No reciprocal or iin house arrangement
Rectification Plan
Trustees prepare a plan to fix the contravention
Auditor Notifies ATO of Contravention Remedy
Auditor informs the ATO upon rectification

Case Study: What Happens When Compliance Fails – Residential Property

An SMSF audited in the past two years revealed several compliance issues with a residential property investment. The fund owned a property in Kearneys Spring, QLD, valued at $455,000. The property was leased to a related party, the trustee's sister, without a formal lease agreement, and the rent charged was not at market rates, creating significant compliance and tax risks. Additionally, leasing to a related party caused the fund to exceed limits on related-party investments, highlighting the importance of proper documentation, market-based rental arrangements, and careful monitoring of related-party transactions to ensure the fund remains compliant and well-governed.

Category	Detail/Findings	Compliance Implications / Trustee Lessons
Property Held	Residential progerty in Kearneys Spring, OLD.	Trustees must ensure the property correctly registered under the corporate trustee.
Valuation	Valued at 8455.000 using an online estimate, no formal independent va-luation	Trustees must obtain an annual market valuation in line with SISR &028. Reliance on unofficial sources increases audit risk.
Lease Arrangements	- Leased to a related party (trustee's sister).- Rent paid aligned with th-ird-party appraisal.	- Absence of lease may result inaidit qualification. - Leasing to related parties can trigger in-house asset breaches and NALI issues.
In-House Asset Rules	- Absence of lease may result in audit qualification.	Trustees must monitor related-party exposures to comply with SISA s.71 & s.82.
SIS Act Breaches	- s.65: Financial assistance to member/ - s.71: Related-party lease createg an in-house asset. - s.82: In-house aset limit exceeded.	Non-compliance may lead to regulatory reporting and corrective action. Demonstrates the consequences of inadequate documantation and non-arm's length tran-sactions.
Regulatory Action	Maintain formal lease agreements, mar-ket valuations, and payment records, en-sure related-party transactions comply w	

Case Study: What Happens When Compliance Fails – Commercial Property

An SMSF invested in a commercial property in Brisbane CBD under a **Limited Recourse Borrowing Arrangement (LRBA)**. The audit identified several compliance issues. The property was recorded at $1,250,000, but no independent or supporting valuation evidence had been obtained for the current year, raising concerns about the accuracy of the fund's reported asset values. Although the tenant was unrelated, the lease agreement was outdated and missing key terms, including escalation clauses and payment schedules, and evidence of rent payments was incomplete, with gaps in bank statements and invoices. In addition, the LRBA loan agreement was not fully documented, and repayments were irregular, creating potential breaches of borrowing rules. This case highlights the importance of maintaining up-to-date valuations, complete lease documentation, reliable payment records, and fully documented borrowing arrangements to ensure compliance and reduce audit and regulatory risk.

Category	Auditor Findings	Compliance Implications / Trustee Lessons
Property Held	Commercial property in Brisbane CBD, purchased via an LRBA.	Trustees must ensure properties are proply recorded and ownership structures comply with regulations.
Valuation	Property recored $1,250,000; no independent or supporting valuation obtained for the current	Trustees should obtain an anniepoendendent valuation or sufficient supporting evidence to demonstrate accura maret value.
Lease Arrangements	Lease agreement outdated; missing escalation clauses and payment schedules.	Maintain up-to-date lease agreements and complete records of rent payments to demonstrate compliance and mitigate audit risk.
LRBA Compliance	LRBA loan agreement not fully documen- repiayments were irregular.	Fully document borrowing arrangements, ensure repayments are made on schedule, and monitor compliancà with borrowing rules to avoid breaches
Key Lesson for Trustees	Inadequate documentation and outdated agreements led to multiple compliance risks,	Proper governance, documentation, and monitoring of property, lease, and borroing arrangements are essential to reduce audit and regulatory risk.

9) Practical Checklist (Trustee Actions)

Right after 30 June

- Order **title search** (dated post year-end).
- Download full-year **bank statements** and **property manager statements**.
- File **rates, insurance** (correct legal name), **invoices**.

Valuation pack (annually)

- Independent valuer OR agent appraisal **with comparable sales.**
- Notes on improvements/market movement.
- For commercial: yield checks; for residential: evidence within 6 months.

Lease & rent

- **Formal lease** on file; for related-party, attach **rental appraisal at commencement/renewal**.
- Rent received **in full and on time**; periodic review documented.

Strategy & structure

- Investment strategy refreshed (diversification/liquidity/risk).
- LRBA loan deed, schedules, and repayment evidence (if applicable).
- Confirm **trustees not disqualified**; auditor **independent & ASIC-approved**.

10. Summary Tables

Audit Requirements: Evidence Needed & Consequences of Non-Compliance

Requirement	Evidence Needed	Consequences of Non-Compliance
Title Search (annual; post-year-end)	Title search confirming correct ownership & no płofh-bired charges (Regulation 13.14)	Audit qualification; possible contravention
Market Valuation (annual)	Current valuation + comparable sales; residential ≤6 months; commercial ≤12...	Modified report; possible ACR
Lease (all properties)	Formal lease; for related-party: rental appraisal at commencement/renewal	Qualification: ACR risk; NALI if over market
Trustee Status	ASIC check: no disqualified persons.	ACR if the disqualified trustee acts.
Auditor Independence	Auditor not involved in fund administration/accounting	Referral to ASIC; loss of approval (auditor)

10.2 Part A / Part B Focus

Audit Components:
Focus Areas & Proving CompliaıCompliance

Component	Focus Area	Regulation / Section	What You Prove
Part A – Financial	Valuation at 30 June	Regulation 8.02B	Evidence supports market value
	Rental income/expenses	–	Completeness, accuracy, allocation
LRBA balances	SIS Act Section 67	SIS Act Section 67	Proper recognition; schedules; repayments
Disclosures	–	–	Property & related-party dealings are transparent
Part B – Compliance		Section 62	Retirement purpose only
Sole purpose test	Sole purpose test	Section 62	Structure compliant
Borrowing rules/LRBA	Borrowing rules/LRBA	Section 67	5% limit observed
In-house asset rules	In-house asset rules	Section 71	5% limit observed
Arm's length	Section 109	Section 109	Commercial terms for rent and dealings
Investment strategy	Regulation 4.09	Regulation 4.09	Documented, reviewed, and suitable
Prohibited charges	Regulation 13.14	Regulation 13.14	No encumbrances

Summary Table of Key Audit Requirements

Requirement | Evidence Needed | Consequences of Non-Compliance

Requirement	Evidence Needed	Consequences of Non-Compliance
Title Search	Title search dated after the audit year end confirming ownership and absence of prohibited charges	Audit qualification if not supplied; possible contravention of SISR 13.14
Market Valuation	Current valuation supported by objective data and comparable sales, Must be obtained on an annual basis	Auditor must modify report and may lodge an ACR if evidence is insufficient, subject to SISR 8.022
Lease Agreement	Formal lease for every property; rental appraisal for related party leases showing market rent	Auditor must lodge ACR if disqualified trustee continues to act – Breach of S17A of SIS Act.
Trustee Status	Evidence trustees are no disqualified via ASIC searh	Auditor must lodge ACR if disqualified trustee continues to act
Auditor Independence	Auditor must be independent; no reciprocal or in house arrangement	Potential referral to ASIC and removal from approved auditor list

Final Thoughts

An SMSF audit is more than a compliance exercise; it is a safeguard that ensures your property investments remain compliant, transparent, and tax-effective. The difference between a trustee who maintains thorough records and one who rushes to find a missing lease or valuation at the last minute is stark.

With the regulatory environment placing increasing emphasis on annual valuations, formal lease agreements, and up-to-date title searches, adopting strong governance practices is no longer optional; it is essential. By staying organised, engaging professional advisers, and following the practical steps outlined in this chapter, you can approach your audit with confidence.

Ultimately, good compliance not only protects your fund from breaches and penalties but also preserves the flexibility and control that make SMSF property investment such a powerful retirement strategy.

RJ's take: "The point of the audit isn't to make life harder, it's to keep your retirement safer. The audit simply confirms what you already know: your SMSF is playing by the rules."

CHAPTER 13: Key Learnings and Final Recommendations for Managing an SMSF

Managing a Self-Managed Super Fund (SMSF) is both an opportunity and a responsibility. It offers trustees flexibility, control, and the potential to grow retirement savings more effectively than traditional superannuation funds. However, it also requires a deep understanding of compliance obligations, investment strategies, and tax efficiencies. Throughout this book, we have covered the critical aspects of SMSF management, from setting up the fund to winding it up, with a special focus on property investments and ensuring long-term financial security.

In this final chapter, we will summarise the key takeaways from the SMSF journey and provide recommendations to help trustees manage their SMSFs effectively, ensuring the best outcomes for their retirement and the retirement of their members.

1. Establishing a Solid Foundation for Your SMSF

The foundation of a successful SMSF lies in proper planning, strong governance, and ensuring compliance from the outset. As a trustee, your responsibility starts from the moment the fund is created, and the decisions you make at the beginning will have a long-lasting impact on the fund's performance.

a) Importance of the Trust Deed and Investment Strategy

The trust deed is the governing document of your SMSF. It defines the powers of the trustees and sets the rules for managing the fund. Ensuring that your trust deed is well-drafted and up-to-date with superannuation laws is crucial for avoiding compliance issues.

Equally important is the investment strategy. Trustees must regularly review and update the investment strategy to reflect the fund's risk tolerance, liquidity needs, and investment objectives. A well-designed investment strategy ensures that the fund is positioned to grow while meeting the needs of its members at every stage of life.

Establishing a Strong Foundation

Establishing a Strong Foundation	Recommendations
Trust Deed	Ensure the trust deed is comprehensive and regularty updated.
Investment Strategy	Formulate a strategy and allocation
LRBA balances	Proper recognition; schedules; repayments
Disclosures	Property & related-party dealings are transparent
Part B – Compliance	Section 62
Sole purpose test	Section 62
Borrowing rules/LRBA	Section 67
In-house asset rules	Section 71

2. Leveraging Property for Long-Term Growth and Income

Property has played a central role in many of the strategies discussed in this book, as it offers SMSFs a unique combination of long-term capital growth and income generation. However, property investments must be carefully managed, especially in relation to *Limited Recourse Borrowing Arrangements* (LRBAs), liquidity, and compliance with the *Sole Purpose Test.*

a) Managing Property Effectively

Property investments in an SMSF require a long-term perspective. Trustees must ensure that properties generate stable rental income and that maintenance costs, property management fees, and loan repayments (if applicable) are covered by the fund's cash flow. It's essential to maintain sufficient liquidity alongside property investments to meet pension obligations and ongoing expenses.

- **Recommendation:** Maintain a balance between property and other liquid investments, such as cash and shares, to ensure the fund has the flexibility to meet short-term liabilities.

b) Taking Advantage of Tax-Free Capital Gains in the Pension Phase

One of the key advantages of property investments within an SMSF is the ability to realise capital gains tax-free during the pension phase. Trustees should plan the timing of property sales strategically to take full advantage of the $1.9 million transfer balance cap, ensuring that gains are maximised without incurring tax liabilities.

Maximising Property Returns

Maximising Property Returns	Recommendations
Balance Liquidity and Property	Diversify with liquid assets to manage short-term liabilities.
Tax-Free Capital Gains	Sell property during the pension phase to benefit from tax-free capital gains.

3. Navigating Tax Efficiencies for Optimal Growth

Tax efficiency is one of the greatest benefits of operating an SMSF. Trustees have access to concessional tax rates, opportunities to manage capital gains tax (CGT), and the ability to claim deductions for fund expenses. By understanding the tax rules applicable to superannuation, trustees can significantly enhance their fund's performance and minimise tax liabilities.

a) Accumulation and Pension Phase Tax Benefits

In the accumulation phase, SMSF earnings are taxed at 15%, and trustees can reduce this through deductions, franking credits, and depreciation on property. However, the real tax advantage lies in the pension phase, where all investment income, including rental income and capital gains, becomes tax-free.

- **Recommendation:** Trustees should carefully plan the transition from accumulation to pension, taking full advantage of the tax-free status in the pension phase by timing asset sales and pension payments appropriately.

b) Utilising the Transfer Balance Cap

The $2 million transfer balance cap sets a limit on how much can be transferred into a tax-free pension account. By planning contributions and withdrawals strategically, trustees can maximise the fund's tax efficiency while ensuring they stay within this cap.

- **Recommendation:** Work with an SMSF adviser to ensure that contributions, pension payments, and capital gains are managed efficiently to stay within the $2 million cap.

Maximising a Property Returns

Maximising Property Returns	Recommendations
Balance Liquidity and Property	Diversify with liquid assets to manage short-term liabilities.
Tax-Free Capital Gains	Sell property during the pension phase to benefit from tax-free capital gains.

Optimising SMSF Tax Efficiency

Optimising SMSF Tax Efficiency	Recommendations
Accumulate Wealth in a Concessional Tax Environment	Plan the transition to the tax-free pension phase to maximise earnings.
Manage the $2 Million Transfer Balance Cap	Use professional guidance to ensure efficient use of the pension balance cap.

4. Maintaining Compliance and Governance

Compliance is an ongoing responsibility for SMSF trustees. Non-compliance can result in significant penalties, including the loss of concessional tax treatment. Trustees must stay up-to-date with changing superannuation regulations and ensure that the fund operates in accordance with the *Sole Purpose Test*, *Arm's Length Rule*, and Regulation 4.09A of the SIS Regulations.

a) Regular Reviews of the Investment Strategy

Regulation 4.09A of the SIS Regulations requires that trustees review and update the SMSF's investment strategy regularly. Trustees must consider risk, diversification, and the fund's liquidity needs to ensure that the strategy remains appropriate as members approach retirement or as the economic environment changes.

- **Recommendation:** Conduct annual reviews of the investment strategy, making adjustments when necessary to ensure the SMSF is aligned with members' retirement goals.

b) Meeting Reporting and Audit Obligations

SMSFs are required to submit an annual return and undergo an annual audit to ensure that the fund remains compliant. Trustees should maintain accurate records, including property valuations, rental agreements, and financial statements, to ensure that audits run smoothly.

- **Recommendation:** Engage with qualified SMSF professionals to ensure that all compliance requirements are met, reducing the risk of penalties or non-compliance.

Ensuring Compliance and Good Governance

Ensuring Compliance and Good Governance	Recommendations
Regularly Review the Investment Strategy	Update the strategy annually or after significant changes in the fund.
Meet Reporting and Audit Obligations	Maintain accurate records and engage qualified auditors to ensure compliance.

5. Planning for the End: Exit Strategies and Winding Up

There will come a time when trustees need to wind up the SMSF. This may occur when members no longer wish to manage the fund, or when the fund becomes too costly to maintain. Having a clear exit strategy in place ensures a smooth transition when it's time to close the SMSF.

a) Selling or Transferring Assets

When winding up an SMSF, all assets must be sold or transferred to beneficiaries. This includes property, shares, and other investments. Trustees should consider the timing of asset sales to minimise CGT (if applicable) and maximise the tax-free status of gains in the pension phase.

- **Recommendation:** Plan the sale or transfer of assets carefully, taking advantage of the tax-free pension phase to avoid unnecessary tax liabilities.

b) Distributing Member Benefits

Before winding up the SMSF, all member benefits must be paid out, either as a lump sum or rolled over into another super fund. Trustees must ensure that death benefit nominations are respected and that beneficiaries receive their entitlements according to the SMSF's trust deed.

- **Recommendation:** Engage with beneficiaries early in the winding-up process to ensure that distributions are handled smoothly and all obligations are met.

Planning for Exit and Winding Up

Planning for Exit and Winding Up	Recommendations
Selling or Transferring Assets	Time for the sale or transfer of assets for optimal tax outcomes.
Distributing Benefits	Ensure that all benefits are distributed according to the trust deed and death benefit nominations.

Final Thoughts

Managing an SMSF is a rewarding but complex responsibility. It requires trustees to stay informed, compliant, and proactive in managing investments. By following the strategies outlined in this book, whether investing in property, maximising tax efficiencies, or planning for retirement, trustees can create a sustainable and successful SMSF that supports its members throughout their lives and into retirement.

The keys to SMSF success are compliance, long-term planning, and diversification. With careful management, SMSF trustees can take control of their retirement savings, grow wealth effectively, and achieve financial security for themselves and their families.

CHAPTER 14: Reference Section for SMSF Management

1. **Trust Deed:** The governing document of the SMSF that must be regularly updated to reflect superannuation laws.
2. **Investment Strategy Compliance (SIS Regulations Regulation 4.09A):** Trustees must regularly review the investment strategy, considering risk, diversification, and liquidity.
3. **Exit and Winding Up Strategies:** Trustees must plan asset sales and distribute benefits appropriately when winding up the SMSF.

Sources and References

This section provides a list of sources and key legal references used throughout this book to help trustees and members manage their SMSFs effectively.

1. Superannuation Industry (Supervision) Act 1993 (SIS Act)

- **Sole Purpose Test (Section 62):** Ensures that SMSFs are maintained solely to provide retirement benefits to members.
- **Arm's Length Rule (Section 109):** Requires SMSF transactions, including property dealings, to be conducted at market value.
- **In-House Asset Rules (Section 71):** Limits the percentage of the fund's assets that can be invested in related-party transactions.

Limited Recourse Borrowing Arrangements (LRBAs) (Section 67A & 67B): Outlines the rules for borrowing within an SMSF to purchase assets like property.

2. Superannuation Industry (Supervision) Regulations 1994

Investment Strategy Compliance (Regulation 4.09A): Mandates that SMSF trustees must formulate and regularly review their investment strategy, considering risk, return, diversification, and liquidity.

3. Australian Taxation Office (ATO) SMSF Guidelines

ATO SMSF Guidelines: The ATO provides guidance on the legal and tax obligations for SMSF trustees. For more information, visit the official ATO website: https://www.ato.gov.au/Super/Self-managed-super-funds

ATO SMSF Wind-Up Procedures: Guides SMSF trustees on the necessary steps and forms required when winding up an SMSF.

4. My SMSF - Self-Managed Super Fund Services

For professional assistance with setting up, managing, and winding up your SMSF, contact My SMSF. They provide expert guidance on SMSF investment strategies, tax compliance, and property investment within an SMSF.

- **Phone:** 1300 545 516
- **Website:** www.mysmsfproperty.com.au

5. Property and Real Estate Sources

- **Realestate.com.au:** For up-to-date data on property prices, rental yields, and trends across different Australian property markets, visit www.realestate.com.au.

This site provides valuable insights for SMSF trustees considering property investments in both residential and commercial markets.

6. Capital Gains Tax (CGT) Guidelines

For details on capital gains tax (CGT) rules applicable to SMSFs, including the one-third discount on capital gains for assets held for more than 12 months, and CGT exemptions in the pension phase, visit:

- **ATO CGT Overview:** https://www.ato.gov.au

7. ASIC SMSF Guides

The Australian Securities and Investments Commission (ASIC) provides guidelines and warnings related to SMSF management, ensuring that trustees understand their responsibilities and risks:

- **ASIC SMSF Information:** https://asic.gov.au

SOURCES AND REFERENCES

This section provides comprehensive sources and references used throughout this book to help trustees and members manage their SMSFs effectively and stay current with regulatory changes.

PRIMARY LEGISLATIVE SOURCES

Superannuation Industry (Supervision) Act 1993 (SIS Act)

- **Section 62: Sole Purpose Test:** Ensures SMSFs are maintained solely to provide retirement benefits
- **Section 66: Related Party Rules:** Governs transactions between SMSFs and related parties
- **Sections 67A & 67B: Limited Recourse Borrowing Arrangements:** Rules for SMSF borrowing
- **Section 71: In-House Asset Limits:** Restricts related party investments to 5% of fund assets
- **Section 109: Arm's Length Transactions:** Requires market-rate dealings for all SMSF transactions
- **Access:** legislation.gov.au

Superannuation Industry (Supervision) Regulations 1994

- **Section 4.09A: Investment Strategy Requirements:** Mandates the formulation and review of SMSF investment strategies
- **Regulations 13.22A-13.22C:** Limited Recourse Borrowing Arrangement provisions

PRIMARY REGULATOR

Australian Taxation Office (ATO): Primary SMSF Regulator

The ATO is the primary regulator for Self-Managed Super Funds, responsible for oversight, compliance monitoring, and enforcement.

Key ATO Resources:

- **SMSF Guidelines:** Comprehensive guidance on legal and tax obligations
  Website: ato.gov.au/Super/Self-managed-super-funds
- **Taxation Ruling TR 2010/1:** Income tax and fringe benefits tax treatment of superannuation contributions
- **SMSF Determination SMSFD 2008/3:** Limited recourse borrowing arrangements

Annual Updates and Rates:

- **Safe Harbour Interest Rates:** Published annually (May/June) for related party loans
- **Superannuation Contribution Caps:** Updated annually for concessional and non-concessional limits
- **Transfer Balance Cap:** Current limits and indexation information
- **Minimum Pension Payment Rates:** Age-based percentage requirements
- **ATO Contact:** 13 10 20 (General Enquiries) | 13 28 61 (Business and Tax Agent Line)

OTHER REGULATORY BODIES

Australian Securities and Investments Commission (ASIC)

- **SMSF Guidance:** Regulatory oversight and consumer protection information
- **Website:** asic.gov.au
- **Focus Areas:** SMSF warnings, compliance monitoring, and industry regulation

Australian Prudential Regulation Authority (APRA)

- **Superannuation Statistics:** Industry data and performance benchmarks
- **Website:** apra.gov.au

MARKET DATA AND RESEARCH SOURCES

Property Market Information

- **CoreLogic:** Property data, market trends, and suburb analysis
  Website: corelogic.com.au
- **SQM Research:** Rental yield data and vacancy rates
  Website: sqmresearch.com.au
- **Real Estate Institute of Australia (REIA):** Market reports and statistics
  Website: reia.com.au

Cryptocurrency Market Data

- **Coin Gecko:** Cryptocurrency prices and market capitalisation
  Website: coingecko.com
- **Coin Market Cap:** Digital asset market data and analysis
  Website: coinmarketcap.com

CRYPTOCURRENCY LENDING PLATFORMS

Block Earner (Australia)

- **Website:** blockearner.com
- **Services:** Bitcoin-backed property loans, cryptocurrency custody
- **Regulatory Status:** Federal Court victory over ASIC (under appeal)
- **Customer Support:** Available through website contact

Ledn (Global)

- **Website:** ledn.io
- **Services:** Bitcoin-backed loans, cryptocurrency savings accounts
- **Custody Partner:** BitGo institutional custody
- **Geographic Coverage:** Global operations with AUD loan options

PROFESSIONAL SERVICES

My SMSF: Specialist SMSF Services

For comprehensive SMSF setup, management, and property investment guidance:

- **Phone:** 1300 545 516
- **Website:** mysmsfproperty.com.au
- **Services:** SMSF establishment, property investment strategies, and ongoing compliance

Legal and Compliance Support

Readers should seek qualified legal guidance from:

- **SMSF specialist lawyers:** For trust deed preparation and compliance matters
- **Superannuation law practitioners:** For complex regulatory interpretation
- **Financial services legal advisers:** For lending and borrowing arrangements

TECHNICAL AND RESEARCH PUBLICATIONS

Academic Sources

- **Australian Centre for Financial Studies (ACFS):** Research on superannuation and retirement
- **Melbourne Institute:** Economic analysis and policy research
- **Reserve Bank of Australia (RBA):** Economic data and financial system analysis

Industry Publications

- **SMSF Adviser Magazine:** Industry news and technical updates
- **Super Guide:** Consumer-focused superannuation information
- **Financial Planning Magazine:** Professional insights and market analysis

STATE GOVERNMENT RESOURCES

Stamp Duty and Property Transfer Information

- **NSW Revenue:** revenue.nsw.gov.au
- **VIC State Revenue Office:** sro.vic.gov.au
- **QLD Office of State Revenue:** osr.qld.gov.au
- **WA Department of Finance:** finance.wa.gov.au

Planning and Development Authorities

- **State planning departments:** For subdivision and development approvals
- **Local councils:** Zoning information and development applications

MARKET ANALYSIS AND COMMENTARY

Financial Markets

- **Australian Financial Review:** afr.com
- **The Australian:** Business and financial news

- **Bloomberg Australia:** Financial markets and economic data

Property Analysis

- **Property Observer:** propertyobserver.com.au
- **Your Investment Property:** Investment strategy and market analysis
- **API Magazine:** Property investment insights

ONGOING COMPLIANCE MONITORING

Regulatory Updates

- **ATO SMSF Newsletter:** Regular compliance updates and guidance
- **ASIC Regulatory Guide Updates:** Changes to financial services regulation
- **Federal Budget Papers:** Annual superannuation changes and announcements

Professional Development

- **Tax Institute:** Continuing professional education
- **Professional accounting bodies:** Technical updates and training

IMPORTANT DISCLAIMERS

Information Currency

All information in this book is current as of the 2024-25 financial year. Readers should verify current rates, caps, and regulations as these change annually. The author recommends checking ATO publications each May/June for updated safe harbour rates and contribution caps.

Professional Guidance Requirement

This book provides general information only. Readers must obtain professional guidance specific to their circumstances from:

- Licensed financial advisers
- Qualified SMSF accountants
- Legal practitioners specialising in superannuation law
- Registered tax agents

Regulatory Changes

Superannuation law is subject to regular changes through:

- Federal Budget announcements
- Legislative amendments
- ATO administrative changes
- Court decisions affecting interpretation
- **Stay Updated:** Subscribe to ATO SMSF updates and professional association newsletters for timely information on regulatory changes affecting SMSF property investment strategies.

General Information Disclaimer

The information contained in this book is provided for general informational purposes only and should not be considered financial, legal, or tax guidance. While every effort has been made to ensure the accuracy of the information presented, readers should be aware that superannuation laws, tax regulations, and other legal requirements are subject to change. The content of this book is based on the laws and practices applicable as of 2024-25.

Consult Professional Guidance

Readers are strongly encouraged to seek professional guidance tailored to their individual circumstances before making any financial decisions. This includes consulting with:

A licensed financial adviser or SMSF specialist,

A qualified accountant or tax adviser, and

A legal professional experienced in superannuation law and estate planning.

The author, publisher, and related parties disclaim any liability for loss or damage arising from reliance on the information contained in this book. Decisions regarding SMSF investments, tax strategies, and compliance should be made in consultation with relevant professionals to ensure that they meet current legal standards and suit your personal financial objectives.

No Warranties

The information in this book is provided "as is," without any representations or warranties, express or implied. The author and publisher make no representations or warranties in relation to the completeness, accuracy, or suitability of the information provided.

Made in the USA
Monee, IL
05 November 2026

67988025R00164